**PILIPINO/ENGLISH
ENGLISH/PILIPINO
CONCISE DICTIONARY**

Also available from Hippocrene...

Pilipino-English/English-Pilipino Dictionary and Phrasebook

by Raymond P. Barrager & Jesusa V. Salvador

No visit to the Philippines can be as rewarding as one where the visitor has experienced first hand the warm hospitality of one of Asia's most enchanting countries. The ability to speak just a few words and phrases may be the key to unlocking the doors to the beautiful Philippine islands.

Combining the benefits of both a dictionary and phrasebook, this pocket-size volume provides the student or traveler with a basis for simple conversation. The dictionary supplies the necessary words to get around in this Asian paradise, while the phrasebook offers sections ranging from accommodations to colloquial expressions. A brief description of Pilipino grammar is also provided.

Pilipino, spoken by well over 10 million people, is the most developed and widely understood of the 8 main Philippine languages.

120 pages • 3¾ x 7 • 0-7818-0451-5 • W • $11.95pb • (295)

PILIPINO/ENGLISH
ENGLISH/PILIPINO
CONCISE DICTIONARY

by

Sam & Angelina Bickford

HIPPOCRENE BOOKS
New York

APPRECIATION-*PASASALAMAT*

We would like to express our appreciation to Connie Litonjua, Ricardo Litonjua, and Jaime Hernandez for their loyal and enthusiastic assistance in the production and editing of this work.

Maraming salamat.

For information, address:
HIPPOCRENE BOOKS, INC.
171 Madison Avenue
New York, NY 10016

ISBN 0-87052-491-7

Printed in the United States of America.

CONTENTS

In memory of
Jose Dionisio
and
Raymunda David

Part I

PILIPINO/ENGLISH

aalis na ako /ah-ah-LIHSS nah ah-KOH/ ex. good-bye

abakada /ah-buh-KAH-duh/ n. alphabet

abala /uh-BAH-luh/ n. disturbance, nuisance

abalahin /ah-bah-LAH-hinn/ v. annoy, disturb, bother

abang /AH-bahng/ v. await, anticipate

abo /ah-BOO/ n. ash

Abril /ah-BREEL/ n. April

abubot /ah-BOO-boat/ n. article, item

abuhin /uh-BOO-hinn/ adj. gray

abutan /ah-BOO-tahn/ v. hand, reach

abutin /ah-BOO-tinn/ v. reach to, amount to, extend

aking /AH-kihng/ prn. mine, my

akitin /ah-KEET-ihn/ v. attract, charm, entice

aklas /ahk-LAHSS/ v. resist

aklasan /ahk-LAHSS-ahn/ n.
  strike, resistance
aklat /ahk-LAHT/ n. book
aklatan /ahk-LAHT-ahn/ n.
  library
ako /uh-KOH/ prn. I
aksaya /ahk-sah-YAH/ n. waste
akyat /ahk-YAHT/ n. climb
akyatan /ahk-YAH-tahn/ n.
  ladder
akyatin /ahk-yah-TIHN/ v.
  scale, board, climb
agad /uh-GAHD/ adv. imme-
  diately
agahan /ah-guh-HAHN/ n.
  breakfast
agamahan /ah-guh-MAH-hahn/
  n. religion
agham /ahg-HAHM/ n. science
agos /AH-gohs/ n. current,
  flow
Agosto /ah-GOHS-toh/ n. August
agwat /ahg-WAHT/ n. distance,
  interval

ahas /AH-hahs/ n. snake
ahente /ah-HAYN-tey/ n.
  salesman, agent
ahit /AH-hit/ n. shave
ahitan /ah-HEE-tahn/ v.
  shave
alak /AH-lahk/ n. wine,
  liquor
alaga /uh-LAH-gah/ n. pet,
  ward, protege
alagaan /ah-luh-GAH-ahn/
  v. take care of
alahas /uh-LAH-hahs/ n.
  jewelry
alalahanin /ah-luh-luh-
  HAH-neen/ v. remember
alalaong baga /ah-lah-lah-
  OHNG buh-GAH/ ex. that is
alam /uh-LAHM/ v. know
alang-alang /AH-lahng AH-
  lahng/ n. sake
alapaap /ah-luh-PAH-ahp/
  n. cloud
alayan /uh-LIE-ahn/ v.
  offer

ale /AH-lay/ n. lady
alikabok /ah-lee-kah-BOKE/
  n. dust
alila /uh-LEE-luh/ n. maid,
  servant
alin /ah-LEEN/ int. which
aling /AH-lihng/ ref. lady
alinlangan /ah-leen-LAHNG-
  ahn/ n. doubt
alinsunod /ah-leen-SOO-
  node/ adv. accordingly
alipin /ah-LEEP-ihn/ n.
  slave
alipustain /ah-lee-poos-
  tah-IHN/ v. slight,
  belittle
alis /ah-LEES/ v. remove,
  leave, depart, take away
aliw /ah-LIEU/ n. comfort
aliwalas /ah-lee-WAHL-ahs/
  adj. spacious
aliwaswas /ah-lee-wahs-
  WAHS/ adj. problemmatic
aliwin /ah-lieu-IHN/ v.
  comfort, solace

alok /ah-LOHK/ n. offer
alon /AH-lohn/ n. wave
alsa /ahl-SAH/ n. rise
alsahin /ahl-sah-HINN/ v.
  raise, lift
alukin /ah-loo-KIHN/ v. offer
ama /ah-MAH/ n. father
amag /AH-mahg/ n. mold,
  mildew
ambon /ahm-BOHN/ n. drizzle,
  light rain, shower
amin /AH-mihn/ prn. our
aminin /ah-MIHN-ihn/ v. admit
amo /AH-moh/ n. boss, head,
  employer
amoy /ah-MOY/ n. smell, odor
ampon /ahm-POHN/ n. adopted
  child, ward
ampunin /ahm-poo-NIHN/ v.
  adopt, assume care of
amukiin /ah-moo-kee-IHN/ v.
  persuade
amuyin /ah-moo-YIHN/ v.
  scent, smell
anak /ah-NAHK/ n. child

ang /ahng/ art. the
angkin /ahng-KIHN/ adj. inborn, intrinsic
angkinin /ahng-kihn-IHN/
  v. claim, lay claim to
angkop /ahng-KOHP/ adj. fit,
  proper, becoming
ani /AH-nih/ n. harvest
anihin /ah-NEE-hihn/ v.
  harvest
anim /AH-nihm/ num. six
animnapu /AH-nihm-nah-POH/
  num. sixty
aninawin /ah-nee-NAH-wihn/
  v. clarify
anino /ah-NEE-noh/ n. shadow
ano /ah-NOH/ int. what
antala /ahn-TAH-luh/ n. delay
antalahin /ahn-tuh-LAH-hihn/
  v. delay
antas /AHN-tahs/ n. degree,
  grade, level
antok /ahn-TOHK/ n. dozing
anyaya /ahn-YIGH-yuh/ n.
  invitation

anyo /ahn-YOH/ n. figure,
 form
anyuin /ahn-yoo-IHN/ v. take
 the form of
aparador /ah-pahr-ah-DOHR/
 cabinet, closet, wardrobe
apat /AH-paht/ num. four
apatnapu /ah-paht-nah-POO/
 num. forty
apawan /ah-PAHW-ahn/ v.
 overfill, overflow
apelyido /ah-pehl-YEE-doh/
 n. surname, family name
apihin /ah-pee-HIHN/ v. mal-
 treat, abuse
apoy /ah-POY/ n. fire
aral /AH-rahl/ n. lesson
aralin /ah-RAH-lihn/ v.
 study
araro /ah-RAH-roh/ n. plow
araruhin /ah-rah-ROO-hihn/
 v. plow
araw /AH-rahw/ n. day, sun
araw-araw /AH-rahw AH-rahw/
 adv. daily, every day

ari /AHR-ih/ n. property
artista /ahr-TEES-tuh/ n.
 movie actor, actress
asa /AH-suh/ v. hope
asahan /uh-SAH-hahn/ n.
 expectation
asal /AH-sahl/ n. behavior,
 manners
asawa /ah-SAHW-uh/ n. wife,
 husband, spouse
asikasuhin /ah-see-kah-SOO-
 hihn/ v. take care of, attend to, keep one's mind on
asim /AH-seem/ n. sourness
asin /ah-SEEN/ n. salt
asinan /ah-seen-AHN/ v. salt
aso /AH-soh/ n. dog
aso /ah-SOO/ n. smoke
aspile /ahs-pee-LIH/ n. pin
asukal /ah-SOO-kahl/ n.
 sugar
asuwang /ahs-WAHNG/ n. witch
at /aht/ conj. and
atay /ah-TIE/ n. liver
ate /AHT-ih/ ref. sister

atin /AH-tin/ prn. our
atubili /ah-too-BEE-lee/
  adj. hesitant, doubtful
awa /AH-wah/ n. pity
awasin /ah-wah-SIHN/ v.
  overflow, take away some
away /AH-wiyh/ n. quarrel
awayin /ah-WIGH-inn/ v. argue, quarrel
awit /AH-wiht/ n. song
awitin /ah-WEET-ihn/ v. sing
ay /iyh/ v. is, are, am
ayaw /AH-yahw/ adj. unwilling; v. dislike
ayon /AH-yohn/ adj. in con-
  formity; adv. according to
ayos /AH-yohs/ n. order,
  arrangement
ayusin /ah-YOOS-ihn/ v. arrange, put in order
ba /bah/ art. indicating a
  question
baba /BAH-buh/ n. chin;
  adj. low, short
baba /buh-BAH/ v. descend

babad /BAH-bahd/ v. soak
babae /bah-BAH-ay/ n. woman
babala /bah-BAH-lah/ n.
 warning
babalaan /bah-buh-LAH-ahn/
 v. warn
babasahin /bah-bah-suh-
 HIHN/ n. reading material
babaw /BAH-bahw/ n. shallow-
ness; adj. shallow
baboy /BAH-boy/ n. pig
baka /BAH-kah/ n. cow
baka /bah-KAH/ adv. perhaps
bakal /BAH-kahl/ n. steel,
 iron
bakasyon /bah-kahs-YOON/
 n. vacation
bakit /BAH-kiht/ int. why
bakla /bahk-LAH/ n. homo-
sexual
bakli /bahk-LEE/ adj. broken
bakod /BAH-kohd/ n. fence
baku-bako /bah-KOO bah-KOH/
 adj. jagged, uneven, rough
bakuran /bah-KOO-rahn/ n.
 yard

baga /BAH-guh/ n. lung
bagal /BAH-gahl/ adj.
 slow, sluggish
bagaman /bah-guh-MAHN/
 conj. although, despite
bagay /BAH-guy/ n. thing;
 adj. becoming, suitable
bago /BAH-goh/ adj. new;
 adv. before
bagsak /bahg-SAHK/ n. fall,
 drop down
baguhin /bah-GOO-hihn/ v.
 change, alter
bagyo /bahg-YOH/ n. storm
baha /buh-HAH/ n. flood
bahaghari /bah-hahg-HAH-
 ree/ n. rainbow
bahagi /buh-HAH-gee/ n.
 part, piece, portion
bahagihin /bah-hahg-EE-
 hihn/ v. divide, apportion
bahagya /bah-hahg-YAH/ adv.
 barely, hardly, scarcely
bahala /buh-HAH-lah/ n. op-
 tion, choice, responsibility

bahay /BAH-high/ n. house
bahid /BAH-hihd/ n. smear
bahin /bah-HIHN/ n. sneeze
baho /BAH-hoh/ n. bad odor,
  stink
bait /bah-ETT/ n. virtue,
  goodness, kindness
bala /BAH-luh/ n. bullet
balaan /bah-LAH-ahn/ v.
  threaten, warn
balabal /bah-LAH-bahl/ n.
  shawl, wrap
balak /BAH-lahk/ n. plan,
  intention
balakang /bah-lah-KAHNG/
  n. hip
balakin /buh-LAHK-ihn/ v.
  plan
balakubak /bah-lah-KOO-bahk/
  n. dandruff
balahibo /bah-lah-HEE-boh/
  n. feather, body hair
balangkas /bah-lahng-
  KAHS/ n. framework
balat /bah-LAHT/ n. skin

balat-kayo /bah-laht kigh-
  YOH/ n. costume, disguise
balbas /bahl-BAHS/ n. beard
balde /bahl-DEE/ n. pail
bali /BAH-lee/ n. fracture,
  break
balik /bah-LIHK/ n. return
balikat /bah-LEE-kaht/ n.
  shoulder
baliktad /bah-lihk-TAHD/
  adj. inside-out, reversed
baligtarin /bah-lihg-tahr-
  IHN/ v. reverse
balino /bah-LEE-noh/ n.
  worry, anxiety
balisa /bah-LEE-suh/ n.
  worry, anxiety
balisa /bah-lee-SAH/ adj.
  restless, worried, anxious
balisahin /bah-lee-SAH-hihn/
  v. agitate, worry
balita /bah-LEE-tuh/ n. news
baliw /bah-LIEU/ adj. crazy
balon /bah-LOON/ n. well
balot /BAH-loht/ n. covering

baluktot /bah-luke-TOHT/
  adj. crooked, bent
balutan /bah-LOO-tahn/ n.
  package, bundle
balutin /bah-LOO-tihn/ v.
  wrap
banal /bah-NAHL/ adj. pious
banayad /buh-NIGH-ahd/ adj.
  moderate, slow, deliberate
bandeha /bahn-DAY-hah/ n.
  tray, platter
bandila /bahn-DEE-luh/ n.
  flag
banga /bah-NGAH/ n. jar
bangka /bahng-KAH/ n. boat
bangkay /bahng-KIYH/ n.
  corpse, cadaver
bangketa /bahng-KAY-tuh/ n.
  sidewalk
bangko /bahng-KOH/ n. bench
banggain /bahng-gah-IHN/ v.
  bump, collide
banggit /bahng-GET/ n. notice, mention
banggitin /bahng-get-IHN/ v.
  mention

bangin /bah-NGIHN/ n. drop,
 precipice, abyss
bangis /bah-NGIHS/ n. wild-
 ness, ferocity
bango /bahng-OH/ n. aroma,
 fragrance
banig /bah-NIHG/ n. mat
banlaw /bahn-LAHW/ v. rinse
banlian /bahn-lee-AHN/ **v.**
 scald
bansa /bahn-SAH/ n. nation
bantay /bahn-TIE/ n. guard
bantayan /bahn-tie-AHN/ **v.**
 guard
bantayog /bahn-TIE-ohg/ n.
 monument
bantog /bahn-TOHG/ adj.
 famous
banyaga /bahn-YAH-guh/ n.
 foreigner
bantot /bahn-TOHT/ n. stink
banyo /BAHN-yoh/ n. bathroom
baol /bah-OHL/ n. trunk,
 chest, footlocker
baon /BAH-ohn/ n. provisions

bapor /bah-POHR/ n. ship
bara /bah-RAH/ n. obstruc-
 tion, blockage
barkada /bahr-KAH-duh/ n.
 gang
barko /BAHR-koh/ n. ship
baril /bah-REEL/ n. gun
bariles /bah-REE-lace/ n.
 barrel
baro /BAH-roh/ n. clothes
barung-barong /BAH-roong
 BAH-rohng/ n. shack, hut
barya /bahr-YAH/ n. change,
 loose coins
baryo /BAHR-yoh/ n. village
basa /bahs-AH/ adj. wet
basa /BAHS-uh/ v. read
basag /BAH-sahg/ adj. broken
basag-ulo /bah-sahg OO-loh/
 n. violence, altercation
basahan /bah-SAH-hahn/ n.
 rag
basahin /bah-SAH-hihn/ v.
 read
basain /bah-sah-IHN/ v. wet

baso /BAH-soh/ n. drinking
 glass, water glass
basta /bahs-TAH/ adv. just,
 merely, simply, enough
baston /bahs-TOHN/ n. cane
bastos /bahs-TOHS/ adj. rude
basura /bah-SOO-ruh/ n.
 trash, garbage
ba't /baht/ int. why
bata /BAH-tah/ n. gown, robe
bata /BAH-tuh/ n. child;
 adj. young
batas /bah-TAHS/ n. law
batayan /bah-TIE-ahn/ n.
 basis, foundation
bathala /baht-HAH-lah/ n. God
bati /BAH-tih/ n. greeting
batid /bah-TIHD/ v. learn
batiin /bah-TEE-ihn/ v.
 greet
batis /BAH-tihs/ n. brook,
 spring, creek
bato /bah-TOH/ n. stone
batok /BAH-tohk/ n. nape
batya /baht-YAH/ n. tub

bawal /BAH-wahl/ adj. illegal, prohibited
bawang /BAH-wahng/ n. garlic
bawas /BAH-wahs/ n. reduction, decrease
bawasan /bah-WAH-sahn/ v. reduce, diminish
bawa't /BAH-waht/ prn. each
bawi /BAH-wee/ n. recovery
bayad /BUY-ahd/ n. payment
bayan /BUY-ahn/ n. country
bayani /buy-AH-nee/ n. hero
bayaran /bah-YAHR-ahn/ v. pay
bayawak /bah-YAH-wahk/ n. lizard
baywang /bay-WAHNG/ n. waist
bentilador /ben-tihl-ah-DOOR/ n. electric fan
bestida /bes-TEE-duh/ n. woman's dress
bibi /BEE-bee/ n. duck
bibig /bee-BIHG/ n. mouth
bikas /BEE-kahs/ n. likeness, appearance
bigas /bee-GAHS/ n. rice

bigat /bee-GAHT/ n. weight
bigay /bee-GUY/ v. give
bigkasin /bihg-kahs-IHN/
v. pronounce, recite
bigkisin /bihg-kihs-IHN/
v. bundle, tie in a bundle
bighani /bihg-HAH-nee/ n.
charm, attraction
bigla /bihg-LAH/ adj. sud-
den; adv. suddenly
biglain /bihg-lah-IHN/ v.
surprise, shock
bigo /bee-GOH/ n. failure,
disappointment; adj. dis-
appointed
biguin /bee-goo-IHN/ v.
disappoint
bihasahin /bee-hah-SAH-
hihn/ v. become accustomed
to, accustom
bihira /bee-HIHR-uh/ adv.
rare, seldom, infrequent
bihis /BEE-hihs/ n. attire,
apparel, dress
bihisan /bee-HEE-sahn/ v.
dress

bihon /BEE-hohn/ n. noodle
bilang /BEE-lahng/ n. number
bilangin /bee-LAHNG-ihn/ v.
 count
bilanggo /bee-lahng-GOH/ n.
 prisoner
bilangguan /bee-lahn-GOO-
 ahn/ n. prison
bilasa /bee-lah-SAH/ adj.
 stale
bilhin /bihl-HIHN/ v. buy,
 purchase
bilihin /bih-LEE-hihn/ n.
 merchandise, goods for sale
bilis /bee-LEES/ n. speed
bilisan /bee-lee-SAHN/ v.
 speed
bilog /BEE-lohg/ n. roundness
biloy /BEE-loy/ n. dimple
bilugin /bee-LOOG-ihn/ v.
 round, make circular
binat /BEE-naht/ n. relapse
binata /bee-NAH-tuh/ n.
 bachelor
bingi /bihng-EE/ adj. deaf

bingwit /bihng-WIT/ n. rod, tackle, pole

binhi /bihn-HEE/ n. seed

binhian /bihn-hee-AHN/ v. seed, breed, sprout

binibini /bee-nee-BEE-nih/ ref. miss

binti /bihn-TEE/ n. leg

biro /BEE-roh/ n. joke

bisa /BEE-sah/ n. effect

bisala /bee-SAH-lah/ n. error, mistake

bisig /BEE-sihg/ n. arm

bitag /BEE-tahg/ n. trap, snare

bitaw /bee-TAHW/ n. release

bitbitin /biht-BIHT-ihn/ v. carry

bitin /BEE-tihn/ n. dangling, suspension

bitiwan /bih-TIHW-ahn/ v. release, let go

bituin /bee-TWEEN/ n. star

biyak /bee-YAHK/ n. slice

biyakin /bee-yahk-IHN/ v. slice, cleave

biyaya /bee-YAH-yuh/ n. favor, grace, mercy
biyayaan /bee-yah-YAH-ahn/
v. grace
Biyernes /bee-YAIR-nehs/ n.
Friday
biyuda /BYOO-duh/ n. widow
bobo /BOH-boh/ adj. stupid
bodega /boo-DAY-gah/ n.
warehouse
bola /BOH-lah/ n. ball
bombahin /bohm-bah-HIHN/
v. pump
boto /BOH-toh/ n. vote
bubungan /boo-BOONG-ahn/
n. roof
bubuwit /boo-BWIT/ n. mouse
buka /boo-KAH/ adj. open
bukas /boo-KAHS/ adj. open
bukas /BOO-kahs/ adv.
tomorrow
bukid /BOO-kid/ n. field
buklatin /buhk-laht-IHN/
v. open
buklod /buhk-LOHD/ n. bind

buklurin /buhk-loo-RIHN/
v. bind, tie, unite
buko /BOO-koh/ n. bud
bukod /boo-KOHD/ adj. separate from; prep. besides
bukol /BOO-kohl/ n. swelling
buksan /buhk-SAHN/ v. open, turn on
bukulan /boo-KOO-lahn/ v. swell
budhi /buhd-HEE/ n. conscience
bughaw /buhg-HAHW/ adj. blue
bugnot /buhg-NOHT/ n. exasperation
bugtong /buhg-TOHNG/ n. riddle, puzzle
buhangin /boo-HAHNG-ihn/ n. sand
buhat /BOO-haht/ prep. from, since
buhatin /boo-HAHT-ihn/ v. lift, carry
buhay /BOO-high/ n. life
buhok /boo-HOHK/ n. hair
buhol /boo-HOHL/ n. knot

bula /boo-LAH/ n. foam,
  bubbles
bulak /BOO-lahk/ n. cotton
bulaklak /boo-lahk-LAHK/
  n. flower
bulag /boo-LAHG/ adj. blind
bulagta /boo-lahg-TAH/ adj.
  unconscious
bulati /boo-LAH-tee/ n.
  earthworm
bulilit /boo-LEE-liht/ adj.
  dwarfish, miniature, tiny
bulok /boo-LOHK/ adj. rotten
bulol /boo-LOHL/ adj. stam-
  mering, stuttering
bulong /boo-LOHNG/ n. whisper
bulsa /buhl-SAH/ n. pocket
bulubundukin /boo-loo-buhn-
  DOO-kihn/ adj. mountainous
bulukin /boo-loo-KIHN/ v.
  decay, spoil
bulungin /boo-LOONG-ihn/
  v. whisper
bulwagan /buhl-WAH-gahn/
  n. hall

bulyaw /buhl-YAHW/ n. rebuke, shout, reproach

bulyawan /buhl-yahw-AHN/ v. shout, rebuke, reproach

bumagyo /boo-mahg-YOH/ v. storm

bumahin /boo-mah-HIHN/ v. sneeze

bumalik /boo-mah-LIHK/ v. return, turn back

bumangon /boo-MAHN-gohn/ v. rise, arise, get up

bumara /boo-mah-RAH/ v. obstruct, block

bumoto /boo-MOH-toh/ v. vote

bundok /buhn-DOHK/ n. mountain

bunga /BOONG-ah/ n. result, fruit

bungang-kahoy /buh-ngahng KAH-hoy/ n. fruit

bunton /buhn-TOHN/ n. pile, heap

buntot /buhn-TOHT/ n. tail

bunutin /boo-NOO-tihn/ v. extract, uproot, pull out

bunyi /buhn-YIH/ n. cheer
buo /boo-OH/ adj. entire,
 whole
bura /boo-RAH/ n. erasure
burahin /boo-rah-HIHN/ v.
 erase
burda /boor-DAH/ n. em-
 broidery
burol /boo-ROHL/ n. hill
busabos /boo-SAH-bohs/ n.
 slave
busalsal /boo-sahl-SAHL/
 adj. slovenly, untidy
busisi /boo-SEE-sih/ adj.
 fastidious, particular
buslo /boos-LOH/ n. basket
butas /BOO-tahs/ n. hole
butiki /boo-tih-KIH/ n.
 lizzard
butil /BOO-tihl/ n. kernel,
 grain
butingtingin /boo-tihng-
 tihng-IHN/ v. scrutinize,
 examine closely
buto /boo-TOH/ n. bone, seed

buwan /boo-WAHN/ n. month,
 moon
buwanan /boo-WAH-nahn/ adv.
 monthly, every month
buwaya /boo-WIGH-ah/ n.
 crocodile
buwig /boo-WIHG/ n. bunch,
 cluster
buwis /boo-WIHS/ n. tax
buwisan /boo-wihs-AHN/ v.
 tax
buwisit /boo-WEES-iht/ adj.
 vexing, unlucky, annoying
buwisitin /boo-wihs-EET-
 ihn/ v. annoy, vex
ka /kah/ prn. you (singular)
kaabalahan /kah-ah-bahl-AH-
 hahn/ n. inconvenience
kaaga-agaya /kah-ah-gah ah-
 GUY-ah/ adj. interesting
kaalaman /kah-ah-LAH-mahn/
 n. information
kaayusan /kah-ah-YOOS-ahn/
 n. order, system, arrangement

kababayan /kah-bah-BUY-ahn/
 n. countryman
kabaitin /kah-buy-ETT-ahn/
 n. kindness
kabayanan /kah-buy-AH-nahn/
 n. town, community
kabayo /kah-BUY-oh/ n. horse
kabibi /kah-BEE-bih/ n.
 shell
kabiguan /kah-bee-GOO-ahn/
 n. disappointment
kabihasnan /kah-bee-hahs-
 NAHN/ n. civilization
kabuhayan /kah-boo-HIGH-
 ahn/ n. existence
kabulaanan /kah-buhl-ah-AH-
 nahn/ n. lie, deceit
kabutihan /kah-boo-TEE-
 hahn/ n. well-being
kabuuan /kah-boo-OO-ahn/
 n. total, whole
kabululan /kah-boo-loo-
 LAHN/ n. nonsense
kakaiba /kah-kah-ee-BAH/
 adj. strange, different

kakayahan /kah-kigh-yah-
HAHN/ n. ability
kakila-kilabot /kah-kee-lah
kee-LAH-boht/ adj. awful,
terrible, frightful
kadakilaan /kah-dah-kee-
LAH-ahn/ n. greatness
kadalasan /kah-dah-LAHS-
ahn/ adv. frequently
kadkarin /kahd-kah-REEN/
v. scatter, spread
kagaguhan /kah-gah-GOO-
hahn/ n. foolishness
kagandahan /kah-gahn-DAH-
hahn/ n. beauty
kagat /kah-GAHT/ n. bite
kagatin /kah-gaht-IHN/ v.
bite
kagawad /kah-GAHW-ahd/ n.
member, staff member
kagawaran /kah-gah-WAHR-
ahn/ n. department, bureau
kagaya /kuh-GUY-ah/ adv. as,
like
kaginhawahan /kah-gihn-hahw-
AH-hahn/ n. ease, comfort

kaguluhan /kah-goo-LOO-
hahn/ n. confusion

kahalagahan /kah-hah-luh-
gah-HAHN/ n. value

kahali-halina /kah-hah-LEE
huh-LEE-nah/ adj. pretty

kahapon /kah-HAH-pohn/ adv.
yesterday

kahawig /kah-HAH-wihg/ adj.
similar, reminiscent

kahel /kah-HEHL/ n. orange

kahidwaan /kah-hihd-wah-
AHN/ n. difference

kahinhinan /kah-hihn-HEEN-
ahn/ n. simplicity, in-
genuousness

kahirapan /kah-hee-RAHP-
ahn/ n. difficulty, hard-
ship

kahit /KAH-hiht/ conj. although, despite

kahit ano /KAH-hiht ah-NOH/
adj. whatever

kahit paano /KAH-hiht puh-
AH-noh/ adv. somehow

kahit saan /KAH-hiht sah-
  AHN/ adv. wherever
kahit sino /KAH-hiht SEE-
  noh/ prn. whoever
kahog /KAH-hohg/ v. rush
kahon /kah-HOHN/ n. box,
  drawer
kahoy /KAH-hoy/ n. wood
kahulugan /kah-hoo-loo-
  GAHN/ n. meaning, sig-
  nificance
kahusayan /kah-hoo-SIGH-
  ahn/ n. perfection
kaibahan /kah-eeb-HAHN/ n.
  discrepancy, difference
kaibigan /kah-ee-BEEG-
  ahn/ n. friend
kailan /kah-ee-LAHN/ int.
  when
kailan man /kah-ee-lahn
  MAHN/ adv. whenever
kailangan /kah-ee-LAHNG-
  ahn/ adj. necessary
kailanganin /kah-ee-lahng-
  AH-neen/ v. need

kainan /kah-ee-NAHN/ n.
 banquet, feast
kainin /kah-EEN-ihn/ v. eat
kaisahan /kah-ee-sah-HAHN/
 n. unity
kalaban /kah-LAH-bahn/ n.
 enemy, adversary
kalabasa /kah-lah-BAH-sah/
 n. pumpkin, squash
kalabisan /kah-luh-BEES-
 ahn/ n. excess, overage
kalabog /kah-lah-BOOG/ n.
 crash, thud
kalakal /kah-LAH-kahl/ n.
 merchandise, business
kalakip /kah-LAH-kehp/
 prep. with, enclosed with
kalagan /kah-LAH-gahn/ v.
 undo, unpack
kalagayan /kah-lah-GUY-ahn/
 n. situation, condition
kalagitnaan /kah-LAH-giht-
 NAH-ahn/ n. midway, middle
kalagmitan /kah-lahg-MEE-
 tahn/ n. probability

kalahati /kah-luh-HAH-tee/
n. half
kalan /kah-LAHN/ n. stove
kalangitan /kah-lahng-IH-
tahn/ n. heaven
kalapati /kah-luh-PAH-tee/
n. pigeon, dove
kalas /kah-LAHS/ adj. loose,
untied
kalasag /kah-LAH-sahg/ n.
shield, armor
kalasin /kah-lahs-IHN/ v.
untie, loosen
kalatagan /kah-lah-TAHG-ahn/
n. surface
kalat /kah-LAHT/ adj. widespread, scattered
kalatan /kah-LAHT-ahn/ v.
strew, scatter
kalawang /kah-LAHW-ahng/ n.
rust
kalawit /kah-LAHW-iht/ n.
hook
kalayaan /kah-lie-YAH-ahn/
n. freedom

kalbo /kahl-BOH/ adj. bald
kalkal /kahl-KAHL/ v. scrape
kalembang /kah-LEHM-bahng/
 n. bell
kalesa /kah-LEHS-ah/ n. rig,
 chaise, carriage
kalikasan /kah-lee-KAHS-
 ahn/ n. nature
kaligtasan /kah-lihg-TAHS-
 ahn/ n. safety
kalihim /kah-LEE-hihm/ n.
 secretary
kalimutan /kah-lee-MOO-
 tahn/ v. forget
kaliwa /kah-lee-WAH/ adj.
 left (direction)
kalmot /kahl-MOHT/ n.
 scratch
kalmutin /kahl-moot-EEN/
 v. scratch
kalokohan /kah-loh-KOH-hahn/
 n. tomfoolery, fraud
kaloob /kah-loh-OHB/ n. gift
kalooban /kah-loh-OH-bahn/
 n. inside, interior

kaluluwa /KAH-loo-loo-wah/
  n. soul, spirit
kalupi /kah-LOO-pee/ n.
  pocketbook, wallet
kaluskos /kah-luhs-KOOS/ n.
  rustle, movement
kalusugan /kah-loo-SOO-
  gahn/ n. health
kalutasan /kah-loo-TAHS-
  ahn/ n. solution, remedy
kaluwalhatian /kah-loo-wahl-
  hah-TEE-ahn/ n. glory
kama /KAH-muh/ n. bed
kamaganak /kah-mahg-AH-
  nahk/ n. relative
kamalian /kah-mahl-EE-ahn/
  n. error, mistake
kamatayan /kah-mah-TIE-ahn/
  n. death
kamay /kah-MY/ n. hand
kambal /kahm-BAHL/ n. twin
kambing /kahm-BING/ n. goat
kami /kah-MEE/ prn. we
kamisadentro /kah-mee-sah-
  DEHN-troh/ n. shirt

kamiseta /kah-mee-SAY-tah/
  n. undershirt
kamot /KAH-moht/ n. scratch
kampihan /kahm-pee-HAHN/ v.
  support, back up, side with
kamukha /kah-mook-AH/ v. appear like, resemble
kamutin /kah-MOO-tihn/ v.
  scratch
kanan /KAH-nahn/ adj. right
  (direction)
kani-kanila /kah-nee kah-
  nee-LAH/ v. own
kanila /kah-nee-LAH/ prn.
  their, theirs
kanin /KAH-neen/ n. rice
kanina /kah-NEE-nah/ adv.
  a short while ago, earlier
kanino /kah-NEE-noh/ prn.
  whose, whom
kanluran /kahn-LOOR-ahn/
  n. west
kano /KAH-noh/ n., adj.
  American
kanya /kahn-YAH/ prn. his,
  her, hers, him

kapabayaan /kah-puh-buy-
ah-AHN/ n. neglect
kapag /kah-PAHG/ conj. if,
when, whenever, in case
kapagdaka /kah-pahg-DAH-
kah/ adv. immediately
kapain /kah-pah-IHN/ v.
grope, feel one's way
kapal /kah-PAHL/ n. thickness
kapalaran /kah-pahl-AHR-
ahn/ n. fate, fortune
kapalit /kah-PAHL-iht/ n.
replacement, substitute
kapalitan /kah-pahl-EE-
tahn/ v. replace
kapalyahan /kah-pahl-YAH-
hahn/ n. absence
kapangyarihan /kah-pahng-
yahr-EE-hahn/ n. power,
authority
kaparis /kah-PAHR-ees/ adj.
similar, alike
kapatagan /kah-pah-TAHG-
ahn/ n. plain, plateau

kapatunayan /kah-pah-too-
  NIGH-ahn/ n. voucher
kapayapaan /kah-pah-yah-
  pah-AHN/ n. peace
kape /kah-PAY/ n. coffee
kapilas /kah-PEE-lahs/ adj.
  like, similar
kapiranting /kah-PRAHN-
  ting/ adv. a small amount
kapiraso /kah-PRAH-soh/ n.
  bit, a little bit
kapisanan /kah-pee-SAH-
  nahn/ n. association,
  organization, society
kapitbahay /kah-piht-BAH-
  high/ n. neighbor
kapote /kah-POH-tay/ n.
  cloak, raincoat
kapuwa /KAHP-wah/ prn. both,
  fellow, kindred
karalitaan /kah-rahl-ee-
  TAH-ahn/ n. poverty
karamihan /kah-rah-MEE-
  hahn/ n. plurality
karanasan /kah-rahn-AHS-
  ahn/ n. experience

karangalan /kah-rahng-AH-lahn/ n. reputation, honor
karaniwan /kah-rahn-EE-wahn/ adj. ordinary, usual
karapatan /kah-rah-PAHT-ahn/ n. right, privilege
karayom /kah-RYE-ohm/ n. needle
karera /kah-RARE-ah/ n. race, racing event
karihan /kahr-EE-hahn/ n. restaurant
karimlan /kah-rihm-LAHN/ n. darkness
kariton /kahr-ee-TOHN/ n. cart
karne /KAHR-nay/ n. meat
karugtong /kah-roog-TOHNG/ n. extension, continuation
karunungan /kah-roo-NOONG-ahn/ n. wisdom, knowledge
kasal /kah-SAHL/ n. wedding
kasalan /kah-SAHL-ahn/ n. marriage
kasalanan /kah-suh-LAH-nahn/ n. fault, guilt

kasalukuyan /kah-sah-loo-KOOY-ahn/ adj. present-day, present-time, current

kasama /kah-SAH-mah/ n. companion

kasangkapan /kah-sahng-KAH-pahn/ n. equipment, equipment, tools

kasangkot /kah-sahng-KOHT/ n. accomplice, conspirator

kasangguni /kah-sahng-GOO-nee/ n. advisor

kasanggunian /kah-sahn-goo-NEE-ahn/ n. council, advisory board

kasanlingan /kah-sahn-lihng-AHN/ n. morality

kasapi /kah-SAH-pih/ n. member

kasarinlan /kah-sah-rihn-LAHN/ n. independence

kasayahan /kah-suh-YAH-hahn/ n. fun, festivity

kasaysayan /kah-sigh-SIGH-ahn/ n. history

kaskasin /kahs-kahs-IHN/ v.
wipe, wipe off
kasibulan /kah-see-boo-
LAHN/ n. youth
kasilyas /kah-SEEL-yahs/ n.
toilet, bathroom
kasintahan /kah-sihn-TAH-
hahn/ n. sweetheart
kasiya /KASH-ah/ adj. satisfactory, sufficient
kasiyahan /kah-see-yah-
HAHN/ n. satisfaction
kasu-kasuan /kah-SUE kah-
sue-AHN/ n. joint
kasulatan /kah-sue-LAH-
tahn/ n. document, writing
kasunduan /KAH-soon-doo-
AHN/ n. contract
kasunod /kah-soo-NOHD/ adj.
next
katabi /kah-tuh-BEE/ prep.
beside
katakawan /kah-tah-KAHW-
ahn/ n. greed
katad /KAH-tahd/ n. leather

katahimikan /kah-tah-hee-
MEE-kahn/ n. tranquillity
katalunan /kah-tah-LOO-
nahn/ n. loss, setback
katamaran /kah-tah-MAHR-
ahn/ n. laziness, idleness
katapangan /kah-tah-PAHNG-
ahn/ n. bravery, courage
katapatan /kah-tah-PAHT-
ahn/ n. honesty, sincerity
katapusan /kah-tah-poos-
AHN/ n. end, termination
katarungan /kah-tah-roong-
AHN/ n. justice
katawan /kah-tah-WAHN/ n.
body
katawanin /kah-tah-wahn-
EEN/ v. represent
katawa-tawa /kah-tah-WAH
tah-WAH/ adj. funny
katayuan /kah-tie-YOO-ahn/
n. standing, position
katibayan /kah-tee-BUY-ahn/
n. proof, evidence, cert-
ification

katimpian /kah-tihm-pee-AHN/ n. control, restraint

katipunan /kah-tee-POO-nahn/ n. federation

katiwala /kah-tee-WAHL-ah/ n. manager, overseer

katok /kah-TOHK/ n. knock

katotohanan /kah-toh-toh-HAH-nahn/ n. truth, fact

katre /KAH-tray/ n. bed

katukin /kah-too-KIHN/ v. knock, rap

katulad /kah-TOO-lahd/ prep. like, as

katulong /kah-TOO-lohng/ n. helper, maid

katunayan /kah-too-NYE-ahn/ n. reality

katungkulan /kah-toong-KOO-lahn/ n. duty, occupation, responsibility

katutubo /kah-too-TOO-boh/ adj. native, innate, inborn

katuwaan /kah-too-WAH-ahn/ n. fun, merriment

katuwiran /kah-TWEER-ahn/
n. reason, motive, justi-
fication

kaugalian /kah-oo-gahl-EE-
ahn/ n. custom, tradition

kaugnay /kah-oog-NIGH/ adj.
connected, related to

kaugnayan /kah-oog-NIGH-
ahn/ n. relation, con-
nection

kaunlaran /kah-oon-lahr-
AHN/ n. progress

kaunti /KOHN-tay/ adj. few,
little, a little bit

kausapin /kah-oo-SAHP-
ihn/ v. talk to

kawad /KAH-wahd/ n. wire

kawal /KAH-wahl/ n.
soldier

kawalan /kah-wahl-AHN/ n.
destitution, privation

kawali /kah-WAHL-ee/ n.
pan, cooking pan

kawani /kah-WAH-nee/ n.
employee

kawawa /kah-WAHW-ah/ adj.
 wretched, miserable
kaway /kah-WYE/ v. wave the
 hand at someone, wave
kawayan /kah-WYE-ahn/ n.
 bamboo
kay /kay/ prep. for, from,
 to
kaya /KAHY-ah/ adj. able
kaya /kah-YUH/ conj. so,
 therefore
kayamanan /kye-uh-MAHN-
 ahn/ n. wealth, riches
kayasin /kye-AHS-een/ v.
 smooth, smooth out
kayo /kye-OH/ prn. you
 (plural), you all
kaysa /kye-SUH/ adv. than
kayumanggi /kye-oo-mahn-
 GEE/ adj. brown
kayurin /kye-OO-rihn/ v.
 scrape, grate
kibo /kee-BOH/ n. action,
 movement, response
kibot /kee-BOHT/ n. throb

kidlat /kihd-LAHT/ n.
lightning
kilabutan /kee-lah-BOOT-
ahn/ v. tremble
kilala /kee-lah-LAH/ adj.
well-known, known
kilay /KEE-lye/ n. eyebrow
kilos /KEE-lohs/ n. action,
movement, gesture
kilusin /kee-LOOS-ihn/ v.
move, act
kinaawaan /kee-nuh-ahw-AH-
ahn/ v. pity, take pity on
kinalabasan /kee-nuh-lah-
bahs-AHN/ n. result
kinatawan /kee-nuh-tahw-
AHN/ v. represent, act for
kirot /kee-ROHT/ n. pain,
sting
kisap-mata /kih-SAHP mah-
TAH/ n. instant, blink of
an eye, wink
kiskis /kihs-KEES/ v. rub
against something, mill
kisig /KEE-sihg/ adj. comely

kislap /kees-LAHP/ n.
 shine, sparkle
kita /KEE-tah/ n. earnings,
 profit; v. see, encounter
kita /kee-TAH/ prn. us,
 you and I
kitain /kee-TAH-ihn/ v.
 earn, make a profit
kitiran /kee-TEER-ahn/ v.
 shorten, take in, narrow
ko /koh/ prn. I, my, mine
koreo /koh-RAY-oh/ n. post
 office
kotse /KOHT-see/ n. car
kubo /KOO-boh/ n. hut
kubol /koo-BOHL/ n. tent
kuhila /koo-HEE-lah/ n.
 traitor
kuhol /koo-HOHL/ n. snail
kulang /KOO-lahng/ adj. in-
 adequate, not enough
kulay /KOO-lye/ n. color
kulayan /koo-LYE-ahn/ v.
 color
kuling /koo-LING/ v. ring

kulisap /koo-LEE-sahp/ n.
 insect
kulob /koo-LOHB/ n. cover,
 wrapping
kulog /koo-LOHG/ n. thunder
kulubong /koo-loo-BOHNG/ n.
 veil, covering
kulubot /koo-loo-BOHT/ n.
 wrinkle
kulubutin /koo-loo-boot-
 IHN/ v. wrinkle
kulutan /KOO-loo-tahn/ n.
 beauty parlor
kulutin /koo-loo-TIHN/ v.
 curl, set a wave
kumbidahin /koom-bee-dah-
 HIHN/ v. invite
kumirot /koo-mee-ROHT/ v.
 sting, pain
kumot /KOO-moht/ n. sheet,
 blanket
kumpol/koom-POHL/ n. bunch
kumpulin /koom-puhl-IHN/ v.
 cluster, gather together
kumpunihin /koom-poon-ee-
 HIHN/ v. repair, fix

kumustahan /koo-moos-TAH-
  hahn/ n. greeting, welcome
kumustahin /koo-moos-tah-
  HIHN/ v. greet
kundangan /koon-DAHNG-ahn/
  ex. due to, because of
kundi /kuhn-DEE/ ex. if not
  for, except for, if not
kung /koong/ conj. if,
  whether
kung gaano /koong guh-AH-
  noh/ adv. how
kung hindi /koong HIHN-dee/
  adv. otherwise, if not
kung minsan /koong MIHN-
  sahn/ adv. sometimes
kung paano /koong puh-AH-
  noh/ adv. how, by what
  means, in what manner
kunin /KOO-nihn/ v. fetch,
  get, procure
kupkupin /koop-koop-IHN/ v.
  protect, keep safe
kurakot /koo-RAH-koht/ v.
  rummage through, search

kuripot /koo-REE-poht/ adj.
 stingy, frugal
kusang loob /KOO-sahng loh-
 OHB/ adj. voluntary
kusina /koo-SEE-nuh/ n.
 kitchen
kusing /koo-SEENG/ n. half
 cent, half penny
kutkutin /koot-koot-IHN/ v.
 unearth, dig, tunnel
kutsara /koot-SAHR-uh/ n.
 spoon
kutsilyo /koo-CHEEL-yoh/ n.
 knife
kutson /koo-CHONE/ n. cushion
kuwadro /KWAHD-roh/ n.
 painting
kuwan /kwahn/ n. something
kuwarta /KWAHR-tah/ n. money
kuwenta /KWEHN-tuh/ n. bill
daambakal /dah-ahm-BAHK-
 ahl/ n. railroad
daan /dah-AHN/ n. road,
 street; num. hundred
daanan /dah-ah-NAHN/ v. pass

dakila /dah-KEE-luh/ adj.
 great, majestic
dakipan /DAHK-ee-pahn/ n.
 arrest, apprehension
dakipin /dah-kee-PIHN/ v.
 arrest, apprehend
dakmain /dahk-mah-EEN/ v.
 grab, snatch
dako /DAH-koh/ n. direction
dakot /dah-KOHT/ n. handful
dakutin /dah-koot-IHN/ v.
 grasp, seize
daga /duh-GAH/ n. rat
dagat /DAH-gaht/ n. ocean
dagdag /dug-DAHG/ n. incre-
 ment, increase, addition
dagdagan /dug-duh-GAHN/ v.
 increase, add to
dagitab /dah-GEE-tahb/ n.
 electricity
dagsa /dahg-SAH/ n. output,
 profusion
dahan-dahan /DAH-hahn DAH-
 hahn/ adv. slowly, gradually
dahil /DAH-hill/ conj. because

dahilan /dah-heel-AHN/ n.
reason, cause
dahon /DAH-hohn/ n. leaf
daigdig /dah-ihg-DEEG/ n.
world
daing /dah-EHNG/ n. complaint
dala /dah-LAH/ n. load,
luggage, baggage
dalaga /duh-LAH-guh/ n. un-
married woman
dalamhati /dah-lahm-HAH-
tee/ n. sorrow, grief
dalampasigan /dah-lahm-pah-
SEE-gahn/ n. shore, beach
dalangin /dah-LAHNG-ihn/ n.
prayer
dalaw /DAH-lahw/ n. visit
dalawa /dah-lah-WAH/ num.
two
dalawahin /dah-lah-wah-
HIHN/ v. make two, pair
dalawampu /dah-lah-wahm-
POO/ num. twenty
dalawin /duh-LAHW-ihn/ v.
visit, date, call on

dali-dali /duh-LEE duh-LEE/
 adv. quickly, hurriedly
dali-daliin /duh-LEE dah-
 lee-IHN/ v. hasten, hurry
daliri /dah-LEER-ee/ n.
 finger
daliri ng paa /dah-LEER-ee
 nuhng pah-AH/ n. toe
dalisay /dah-LEE-sigh/ adj.
 pure, immaculate
dalo /dah-LOH/ n. attendance
dalos /DAH-lohs/ n. haste
daloy /DAH-lohy/ n. flow
dalubhasa /dah-loob-HAH-
 sah/ n. expert
daluyan /dah-LOO-yahn/ v.
 flow
damahin /dah-mah-HIHN/ v.
 realize
damayan /duh-MY-ahn/ v. sym-
 pathize with, minister to
damdamin /dahm-DAHM-ihn/ n.
 feeling
damhin /dahm-HIHN/ v. feel
dami /DAH-mee/ n. quantity

damo /dah-MOH/ n. grass
dangal /dahng-AHL/ n. honor
dantaon /dahn-tah-OHN/ n.
 century
dapat /DAH-paht/ v. ought,
 should
daplis /dahp-LIHS/ n. miss,
 near hit
daplisan /dahp-lihs-AHN/ v.
 miss, brush
dasal /dah-SAHL/ n. prayer
dasalan /dah-SAH-lahn/ n.
 rosary, prayer beads
dasalin /dah-sahl-IHN/ v.
 pray
datapwa /DAH-tahp-wah/ conj.
 however, but
dati /DAH-tee/ adj. former;
 adv. formerly,
datnin /daht-NIHN/ v. reach,
 arrive to
datu /DAH-too/ n. chieftain
daungan /dah-OONG-ahn/ n.
 wharf, pier, port
daw /dahw/ adv. reportedly

dayain /dye-AH-een/ v.
  swindle, cheat
dayami /dye-AH-mee/ n. hay,
  straw
dayo /DYE-oh/ n. foreigner
dayuhan /dye-OO-hahn/ adj.
  foreign, alien
di /dee/ adv. no, not
dibdib /deeb-DEEB/ n. bosom,
  breast, chest
di-kailanman /DEE kah-ee-
  lahn-MAHN/ adv. never
di-kasiya /dee KAHS-yuh/
  adj. unsatisfactory
di-kaya /dee KYE-uh/ adj.
  unable
digma /dihg-MAH/ n. war
diin /dee-EEN/ n. pressure
diinan /dee-ee-NAHN/ v.
  press
di-inaprubahan /DEE ihn-ah-
  proo-bah-HAHN/ v. disapprove, reject
dila /DEE-lah/ n. tongue
di lata /dee LAH-tuh/ n.
  tin can, canned goods

dilaw /dee-LAHW/ adj. yellow
dilidili /DEE-lee-DEE-lih/
  n. sense, cognition
dilidilihin /dih-LEE-dih-
  LEE-hihn/ v. think
diligin /dih-LIHG-ihn/ v.
  sprinkle, water (plants)
dilim /dih-LEEM/ n. darkness
dilimin /dih-lihm-IHN/ v.
  darken, be overtaken by dark
di-maasahan /DEE-mah-ah-SAH-
  hahn/ adj. unreliable
di-mabilang /DEE-muh-BEE-
  lahng/ adj. numerous
di-nasiyahan /DEE-nah-see-
  yah-HAHN/ adj. discontented
din /dihn/ adv. also, too
dingding /dihng-DIHNG/ n.
  wall
dini /DEE-nay/ adv. here
di-pagkakaunawaan /DEE-pahg-
  kah-kuh-oon-ah-WAH-ahn/ n.
  misunderstanding
di-pantay /DEE-pahn-TIE/
  adj. uneven, not smooth
diri /DEER-ih/ n. loathing

Disyembre /dihs-YEHM-bray/
  n. December
di-tama /dee-TAH-mah/ adj.
  incorrect
dito /DEE-toh/ adv. here
diwa /DEE-wah/ n. spirit
diwata /dee-WAH-tah/ n.
  goddess
diyan /djahn/ adv. there
doblihin /doh-blay-HIHN/
  v. double
doon /dune/ adv. there
dukutin /doo-KOOT-ihn/ v.
  pull out, draw out, remove
dugo /doo-GOH/ n. blood
dugtong /doog-TOHNG/ n.
  extension, annex, addition
dugtungan /doog-toong-AHN/
  v. extend, add to
dula /doo-LAH/ n. drama
dulaan /DOO-lah-ahn/ n.
  theater
dulang /DOO-lahng/ n.
  dining table
duling /doo-LIHNG/ adj.
  cross-eyed

dulo /DOO-loh/ n. end,
  terminal point
dulot /DOO-loht/ n. offer
dulutan /doo-LOOT-ahn/ v.
  offer, propose
dumaan /doo-muh-AHN/ v.
  pass, course through
dumalo /doo-MAH-loh/ v.
  attend
dumaloy /doo-MAH-loy/ v.
  flow
dumanas /doo-MAHN-ahs/ v.
  experience
dumating /doo-mah-TIHNG/ v.
  arrive
dumi /doo-MEE/ n. dirt
dumihan /doo-mee-HAHN/ v.
  dirty, soil
dumugo /doo-moo-GOH/ v.
  bleed
dungo /doong-OH/ adj. timid
dunong /DOO-nohng/ n.
  knowledge
durog /doo-ROHG/ adj. pul-
  verized, crushed, smashed

durugin /doo-ROOG-ihn/ v.
 crush, grind up
duwag /dwahg/ adj. cowardly
duwal /doo-WAHL/ n. vomit
duyan /DOO-yahn/ n. cradle
Enero /ee-NEHR-oh/ n.
 January
eskoba /ehs-KOH-bah/ n.
 brush
eskubahin /ehs-koo-BAH-
 hihn/ v. brush
eto /EH-toh/ ex. here!
ewan /EH-wahn/ ex. I don't
 know
gaan /guh-AHN/ n. ease,
 lightness, easiness
gaanan /gah-ah-NAHN/ v.
 ease, lighten
gabi /gah-BEE/ n. night
gaga /GAH-gah/ n. fool
gahasa /gah-HAH-sah/ v. rape
galak /gah-LAHK/ n. joy
galaw /gah-LAHW/ n. movement
galawin /gah-lahw-EEN/ v.
 move

galgal /gahl-GAHL/ adj.
 used, second-hand
galian /gahl-EE-ahn/ n.
 ceremony
galing /gah-LIHNG/ n. ex-
 cellence, merit, amulet
galing sa /GAH-lihng sah/
 prep. from
galis /gah-LIHS/ n. itch
galit /GAH-liht/ n. anger
galitin /gah-LIHT-ihn/ v.
 anger
gambala /gahm-BAH-lah/ n.
 disturbance
gambalain /gahm-bahl-AH-
 ihn/ v. disturb, delay
gamit /GAHM-iht/ n. use
gamitin /gah-MEET-ihn/ v.
 use, utilize
gamot /gah-MOHT/ n. medicine
gamutan /gah-MOOT-ahn/ n.
 treatment
gamutin /gah-moo-TIHN/ v.
 treat, render treatment
gana /GAH-nah/ n. appetite

ganap /gah-NAHP/ adj. complete, fulfilled

gandahan /gahn-duh-HAHN/ v. decorate, adorn, beautify

ganito /gahn-ee-TOH/ adv. thus, like this

gantimpala /gahn-tihm-PAHL-uh/ n. reward, prize

gantimpalaan /gahn-tihm-pahl-uh-AHN/ v. reward

ganyak /gahn-YAHK/ n. enticement, attraction

ganyan /gahn-YAHN/ adv. like that, thus

gapiin /gah-PEE-ihn/ v. overpower, overcome

gapos /GAH-pohs/ n. manacle

gapusin /gah-POOS-ihn/ v. bind, manacle, tie up

gasgas /gahs-GAHS/ adj. worn out, scratched

gastos /GAHS-tohs/ n. expenses

gata /gaht-AH/ n. juice

gatas /GAH-tahs/ n. milk

gatong /GAH-tohng/ n. fuel
gawa /gah-WUH/ n. work
gawaan /gah-wuh-AHN/ n.
 factory, workshop
gawgaw /GAHW-gahw/ n. starch
gawi /guh-WEE/ n. direction
gaya /GAHY-uh/ n. imitation
gayahin /guy-AH-hihn/ v.
 imitate
gayuma /guy-OO-muh/ n.
 charm, allurement
giba /gee-BAH/ adj. wrecked
gibain /gee-bah-IHN/ v.
 wreck, demolish
gilagid /gee-LAH-gihd/ n.
 gum (of the mouth)
gilalas /gee-luh-LAHS/ n.
 astonishment, wonder
gilid /GEEL-ihd/ n. edge
giniling /gee-NEEL-ihng/ n.
 ground meat, hamburger
ginintuan /gih-neen-too-
 AHN/ adj. golden
ginto /geen-TOH/ n. gold
gising /gees-IHNG/ adj. awake

gisingin /gee-SEENG-ihn/ v.
 awaken
gitgit /giht-GIHT/ v. crowd,
 elbow one's way through
gitla /giht-LAH/ n. shock
gitlahin /giht-luh-HIHN/ v.
 shock, surprise
gitna /giht-NAH/ n. middle
gitnaan /giht-nuh-AHN/ adj.
 middle
goma /GOH-muh/ n. rubber
grabe /GRAH-bay/ adj. critical, serious
guhit /GOO-hiht/ n. line
gulang /GOO-lahng/ n. age
gulat /GOO-laht/ n. surprise
gulatin /goo-LAHT-ihn/ v.
 surprise, shock
gulay /GOO-lie/ n. vegetable
gulo /goo-LOH/ n. unrest
gulong /goo-LOONG/ n. wheel
guluhin /goo-loo-HIHN/ v.
 confuse, complicate
gumanap /goo-mahn-AHP/ v.
 perform, enact, fulfill

gumaod /goo-MAH-ohd/ v. row

gumapang /goo-MAH-pahng/
v. crawl

gumasta /goo-MAHS-tah/ v.
spend

gumawa /goo-muh-WAH/ v. do

gumising /goo-MEE-sihng/
v. wake up

gunamgunam /goo-nahm-GOO-
nahm/ n. meditation

guniguni /goo-NEE-goo-NEE/
n. imagination

gunita /goon-ee-TAH/ n. re-
collection, memory

gunitain /goo-nee-tah-IHN/
v. recall, recollect

gunting /goon-TEENG/ n.
scissors

gupit /goo-PIHT/ n. haircut

gupitan /goo-pih-TAHN/ v.
trim, cut the hair

gusali /goo-SAH-lee/ n.
building

gutom /GOO-tohm/ n. hunger

gutumin /goo-TOOM-ihn/ v.
make one become hungry

guwang /goo-WAHNG/ n.
  hollow, crevice
haba /HAH-buh/ n. length
habang /HAH-bahng/ prep.
  during; conj. while
habiin /hah-BEE-ihn/ v.
  weave
habilin /hah-BEEL-ihn/ n.
  will, testament
habol /HAH-bohl/ v. hurry
  after, try to overtake
habong /HAH-boong/ n. lean-
  to, temporary shelter
haka /HAH-kah/ n. surmise,
  speculation
hakbang /hahk-BAHNG/ n. step
hakot /HAH-koht/ n. load
hakutin /hah-KOOT-ihn/ v.
  load
hadlangan /hahd-lahng-AHN/
  v. obstruct, prevent
hagdan /hahg-DAHN/ n. staircase, stairway, stairs
hagdanan /hahg-dahn-AHN/ v.
  make a ladder, scale
hagibis /hah-gee-BIHS/ v.
  zoom, zip, run fast

hagilapin /hah-gee-LAHP-
 ihn/ v. search for, ransack
hagis /HAH-gihs/ n. throw
hagisan /hah-GEES-ahn/ v.
 throw
hagod /HAH-gohd/ n. rub
hagpos /hahg-POHS/ adj.
 loose
hagulgol /hah-gool-GOHL/
 n. weeping, wail
hagurin /hah-GOO-rihn/ v.
 rub, caress
halakhak /hah-lahk-HAHK/ n.
 laughter
halakhakan /hah-lahk-hahk-
 AHN/ v. laugh
halaga /hah-luh-GAH/ n.
 price, value, worth, amount
halagahan /hah-lah-gah-
 HAHN/ v. price, appraise
halal /hah-LAHL/ n. vote
halalan /HAHL-ah-lahn/ n.
 election
halaman /hah-LAH-mahn/ n.
 plant
halamanan /HAH-lah-mah-
 NAHN/ n. garden

halangan /hah-LAHNG-ahn/ v.
  place an obstacle, fence
halata /hah-lah-TAH/ adj.
  visible, noticeable
halatain /hah-lah-tah-IHN/
  v. find out, bring out
halaw /hah-LAHW/ n.
  translation
halawin /hah-lahw-IHN/ v.
  translate
halik /hah-LIHK/ n. kiss
halika /hah-LAY-kuh/ ex.
  come here
halikan /hah-lee-KAHN/ v.
  kiss
haligi /hah-LEE-gih/ n.
  post, pillar
halimaw /hah-LEE-mahw/ n.
  beast, monster
halimbawa /hah-leem-BAHW-
  uh/ n. example; ex. for
  example
halo /HAH-loh/ n. mixture,
  stir
halos /HAH-lohs/ adv. al-
  most, mostly

haluin /hah-LOO-ihn/ v.
 stir
halumigmig /han-loo-mihg-
 MIHG/ adj. moist
halungkatin /hah-loong-
 kaht-IHN/ v. search for,
 canvass
hamakin /hah-MAHK-ihn/ v.
 belittle
hamog /hah-MOOG/ n. dew
hamon /HAH-mohn/ n. dare,
 challenge
hampasin /hahm-pahs-IHN/
 v. bump, strike
hamunin /hah-MOON-ihn/ v.
 challenge, dare
hanap /HAHN-ahp/ n. hunt,
 search, object of search
hanapbuhay /hahn-ahp-BOO-
 high/ n. livelihood, job
hanapin /hah-NAHP-ihn/ v.
 hunt, look for
hanay /HAH-nigh/ n. row
handa /hahn-DUH/ adj.
 ready, prepared

handog /hahn-DOHG/ n. gift
handusay /hahn-DOO-sigh/
  adj. exhausted, prostrate
hanggahan /hahng-GAH-hahn/
  n. boundary
hangganan /hahng-GAH-nahn/
  n. border, limit
hanggang /hahng-GAHNG/
  prep., conj. until, up to
hangin /HAHNG-ihn/ n. air,
  wind
hapdi /hahp-DEE/ n. pain
hapis /HAHP-ees/ n. agony
hapon /HAH-pohn/ n.
  afternoon
hapunan /hah-POO-nahn/ n.
  dinner, supper
harapan /HAHR-ah-pahn/ n.
  front, public view
hari /HAHR-ee/ n. king
harina /hahr-EE-nuh/ n.
  flour
hati /HAHT-ih/ n. portion,
  share
hatiin /hah-TEE-ihn/ v.
  divide, share

hatinggabi /haht-ihng-guh-
 BEE/ n. midnight
hatol /HAH-tohl/ n. ver-
 dict, decision
hatulan /hah-TOOL-ahn/ v.
 decide, render a verdict
hawak /HAHW-ahk/ n. grasp,
 hold
hawakan /hahw-AHK-ahn/ v.
 hold, grasp
hawla /HAHW-luh/ n. cage
hayaan /high-YAH-ahn/ v.
 allow, let, ignore
hayan /hee-YAHN/ ex. there!
hayop /HIGH-ohp/ n. animal
hikayat /hee-KIGH-aht/ n.
 persuasion
higa /hee-GAH/ v. lie down
higab /hee-GAHB/ n. yawn
higad /HEE-gahd/ n. larva,
 caterpillar
higit /hee-GIHT/ adv. more
higop /HEE-gohp/ n. sip
hilaga /hee-LAH-gah/ n.
 north

hilahin /hee-LAH-hihn/ v.
 drag, pull, tow
hilahod /hee-lah-HOHD/ adj.
 dragging, shuffling along
hilam /HEE-lahm/ n. sting
hilamos /hee-LAH-mohs/ v.
 wash the face
hilamusan /hee-lah-moos-
 AHN/ n. sink, wash basin
hilaw /hee-LAHW/ adj. raw
hilik /hee-LIHK/ v. snore
hilig /HEE-lihg/ n. in-
 clination, tendency
hilingin /hee-leeng-IHN/
 v. petition, demand
hilo /HEE-loh/ n. dizzi-
 ness, faint, nausea
hilom /HEE-lohm/ v. cure,
 heal
hilurin /hee-LOOR-ihn/ v.
 scrub
hilutin /hee-LOOT-ihn/ v.
 rub, massage
himagsikan /hee-mahg-SEE-
 kahn/ n. uprising, tumult

himas /HEE-mahs/ n. caress
himasin /hee-MAHS-ihn/ v.
 pet, caress
himasok /hee-MAHS-ohk/ n.
 interference, meddling
himatay /hee-muh-TIE/ n.
 faint, swoon
himatayin /hee-muh-tie-
 IHN/ v. faint, swoon
himaymay /hee-my-MY/ n.
 strand, fiber
himbing /hihm-BEENG/ n.
 sound sleep, slumber
himig /HEE-mihg/ n. melody
himigan /hee-MEE-gahn/ v.
 compose, create
himpapawid /heem-pah-pah-
 WIHD/ n. air, atmosphere
himpilan /hihm-PIHL-ahn/
 n. stopping point, station
himulmol /hee-mool-MOHL/
 n. strip, plucking
hina /HEE-nuh/ n. weakness
hinaharap /hee-nuh-HAHR-
 ahp/ n. future

hinahon /hee-NAH-hohn/ n.
  calmness
hinahunin /hee-nah-HOO-
  nihn/ v. calm, calm down
hinala /hee-NAHL-uh/ n.
  suspicion, premonition
hinalain /hee-nuh-LAH-ihn/
  v. suspect
hinamak /hee-NAH-mahk/ v.
  humble, put down
hinawakan /hee-nuh-WAHK-
  ahn/ v. hold, grasp
hindi /hihn-DEE/ adv. no,
  not
hinga /hihng-AH/ v. breathe
hingi /hihng-EE/ v. ask,
  request
hininga /hihn-eeng-AH/ n.
  breath
hinlalaki /hihn-lah-lahk-
  EE/ n. thumb
hinog /hee-NOOG/ adj. ripe
hintay /hihn-TIE/ v. wait
hintayan /hihn-TIE-ahn/ n.
  wait, waiting room

hinto /hihn-TOH/ v. stop
hinugin /hee-noog-IHN/ v.
 ripen
hipo /HEE-poh/ n. touch
hipuin /hee-poo-IHN/ v.
 touch
hiram /hee-RAHM/ n. loan
hiramin /hee-rahm-IHN/ v.
 borrow
hirangin /hee-RAHNG-ihn/ v.
 appoint
hirap /HEE-rahp/ n. hardship
hita /HEE-tah/ n. thigh
hititin /hee-tiht-IHN/ v.
 smoke
hiwa /HEE-wuh/ n. slice
hiwaga /hee-WAH-guh/ n.
 mystery
hiwain /hee-WAH-ihn/ v. cut,
 slice
hiwalay /hee-wuh-LIE/ adj.
 separate, apart
hiwalayan /hee-wuh-lie-AHN/
 v. separate
hiya /HEE-yuh/ n. shame, em-
 barrassment, dishonor

hiyain /hee-yah-IHN/ v.
  shame, embarrass
hiyang /hee-YAHNG/ adj.
  agreeable, suitable
hiyas /hee-YAHS/ n. jewelry
hiyaw /hee-YAHW/ n. shout
hiyawan /hee-yahw-AHN/ v.
  shout, yell
ho /hoh/ n. sir, ma'am
hubad /hoo-BAHD/ adj. nude
hubaran /hoo-bahr-AHN/ v.
  undress
hubo /hoo-BOH/ adj. naked
hubog /HOO-bohg/ n. shape
hubugin /hoo-BOOG-ihn/ v.
  shape, form
hukayan /hoo-KIGH-ahn/ n.
  dig, gravesite, excavation
hukayin /hoo-kigh-IHN/ v.
  dig
hukbo /hook-BOH/ n. army
hukom /hoo-KOHM/ n. judge
hukuman /HOO-koo-mahn/ n.
  court
hudyat /huhd-YAHT/ n. sign

hudyatan /huhd-YAHT-ahn/ n.
  password
hudyatan /huhd-yaht-AHN/ v.
  signal
hugasan /hoo-GAHS-ahn/ v.
  wash
hugasan /hoo-gahs-AHN/ n.
  washtub, sink
hugis /HOO-gihs/ n. form,
  outline, shape
hugisan /hoo-GIHS-ahn/ v.
  outline, form, fashion
hugos /HOO-gohs/ n. rush
hugutin /hoo-GOOT-ihn/ v.
  draw out, pull out
hula /HOO-luh/ n. guess
hulaan /hoo-LAH-ahn/ v.
  guess, predict
hulihin /hoo-LEE-hihn/ v.
  catch
hulmahin /hool-mah-HIHN/
  v. pattern, mold
hulog /HOO-lohg/ n. fall,
  installment; v. fall
hulwaran /hool-WAHR-ahn/
  n. pattern, model

Hulyo /HOOL-yoh/ n. July
humigab /hoo-mee-GAHB/ v.
  yawn
humimpil /hoo-meem-PIHL/ v.
  station, position
huminga /hoo-mihng-AH/ v.
  breathe
humiwalay /hoo-mee-wah-
  LIE/ v. part, separate
humpak /hoom-PAHK/ adj.
  hollow
Hunyo /HOON-yoh/ n. June
hurno /hoor-NOH/ n. oven
hurnuhin /hoor-noo-HIHN/ v.
  bake
husto /hoos-TOH/ adj. ap-
  propriate, right, fitting
huwad /hoo-WAHD/ adj. fake,
  counterfeit
huwaran /HOO-wahr-ahn/ n.
huwarin /hoo- wahr-EEN/ v.
  model
Huwebes /hoo-WAY-behs/ n.
  Thursday
huwes /hoo-WEHS/ n. judge
iba /ee-BUH/ adj. other

ibaba /ee-buh-BAH/ adv.
down, below; v. lower
ibabaw /ee-BAH-bahw/ adv.
above; n. top
ibagsak /ee-bahg-SAHK/ v.
drop, let fall
ibalik /ee-bah-LIHK/ v.
return
iba't-ibang /ee-BAHT ee-
BAHNG/ adj. various
ibatay /ee-BAH-tie/ v. base
ibayo /ee-BUY-oh/ adj. double; n. opposite side
ibig /EE-bihg/ n. like,
want
ibigay /ee-bee-GUY/ v. give
ibigin /ee-BEEG-ihn/ v. desire, like, love, want
ibig-sabihin /EE-bihg suh-
BEE-hihn/ n. meaning; v.
mean
ibili /ee-bee-LEE/ v. buy
ibinitiwan /ee-been-ee-
TEEW-ahn/ v. let go of, put
down, lay aside
ibintang /ee-bihn-TAHNG/ v.
accuse

ibitin /ee-BEET-ihn/ v.
 hang up
ibon /EE-bohn/ n. bird
ibuhos /ee-BOO-hohs/ v.
 pour, douse
ibulalas /ee-boo-lah-
 LAHS/ v. cry out, scream
ibunton /ee-boon-TOHN/ v.
 pile up, heap
ika /ee-KAH/ v. limp
ikabit /ee-kuh-BIHT/ v. at-
 tach, connect
ikatlo /ee-kaht-LOH/ adj.
 third
ikaw /ee-KAHW/ prn. you
ikid /EE-kihd/ n. coil,
 twist, roll
ikirin /ee-KEER-ihn/ v.
 coil, roll
ikiskis /ee-kees-KIHS/ v.
 mill, rub together
ikuha /ee-KOO-huh/ v. get
idlip /ihd-LIHP/ n. nap
iduro /ee-DOO-roh/ v.
 prick, penetrate
igat /EE-gaht/ n. eel

igkasin /ihg-KAHS-ihn/
adj. elastic, springy
iginalang /ee-geen-AHL-
ahng/ v. honor, fete
ihain /ee-HAH-ihn/ v. serve
ihalal /ee-hah-LAHL/ v.
elect
ihambing /ee-hahm-BIHNG/
v. compare
ihanda /ee-hahn-DAH/ v.
prepare
ihanga /ee-HAHNG-ah/ v.
admire
iharap /ee-hahr-AHP/ v.
face, come forward
ihatid /ee-hah-TIHD/ v.
escort
ihawin /ee-hahw-IHN/ v.
roast
ihi /EE-hee/ n. urine
ihip /ee-HIHP/ v. blow,
puff
ihulog /ee-HOO-lohg/ v.
send, post
ilakip /ee-LAH-kep/ v. include, enclose

iladlad /ee-lahd-LAHD/ v.
 unfurl
ilag /EE-lahg/ v. avoid
ilagay /ee-luh-GUY/ v.
 place, put
ilalim /ee-LAH-leem/ prep.
 below, under; n. bottom
ilan /ee-LAHN/ adj. some;
 int. how many?
ilaw /EE-lahw/ n. light
ilibing /ee-lee-BIHNG/ v.
 bury
ilista /ee-lihs-TAH/ v.
 note, list, jot down
ilog /EE-lohg/ n. river
ilong /ee-LOHNG/ n. nose
imbak /eem-BAHK/ n. stock,
 reserves
imbakin /eem-bahk-IHN/ v.
 stock up, preserve
imbi /ihm-BEE/ adj. mean,
 petty
imbot /ihm-BOHT/ n. greed
imik /ee-MIHK/ n. talk
imikan /ee-mihk-AHN/ v.
 talk, chat

impitin /ihm-piht-IHN/ v.
 tighten
impok /ihm-POHK/ n. savings
impukin /ihm-pook-IHN/ v.
 save
ina /ee-NAH/ n. mother
inaabangan /EE-nuh-ah-
 bahng-AHN/ v. expect
inaaralan /EE-nuh-ahr-AHL-
 ahn/ n. pupil, student
inamin /ee-nahm-IHN/ v. admit, acknowledge
inat /ee-NAHT/ v. stretch
inayos /een-AHY-ohs/ v.
 process
ingat /EENG-aht/ n. care,
 caution, prudence
ingatan /ihng-AHT-ahn/ v.
 take care, exercise caution
ingat-yaman /EENG-aht
 YAH-mahn/ n. treasurer
ingay /EENG-igh/ n. sound
ingayan /eeng-IGH-ahn/ v.
 make noise
inggit /eeng-GIHT/ n. envy

inggitin /eeng-giht-EEN/
  v. envy
inihulog /ee-nee-HOO-lohg/
  v. mail
inip /ee-NIHP/ adj. im-
  patient
inis /ee-NIHS/ adj. exas-
  perated, irritated
inisin /ee-nihs-IHN/ v.
  irritate, exasperate
init /EE-niht/ n. heat
initin /ee-NEET-ihn/ v.
  heat
intindi /ihn-tihn-DEE/ n.
  understanding, accord
intindihin /ihn-tihn-dee-
  HIHN/ v. notice, mind, pay
  attention to
inubo /een-oo-BOH/ v. cough
inumin /ihn-oo-MIHN/ n.
  drink, beverage
inurong /ihn-OOR-oong/ v.
  recede, pull back, reverse
inutos /ihn-OO-tohs/ v.
  order, command
inyo /ihn-YOH/ adj. your

ipadala /ee-puh-dah-LAH/ v.
 send, deliver
ipagbalita /ee-pahg-buh-
 LEE-tah/ v. advertise
ipagbili /ee-pahg-bee-LEE/
 v. sell
ipagyabang /ee-pahg-YAH-
 bahng/ v. boast, swagger
ipahatid kawad /ee-puh-hah-
 TIHD KAH-wahd/ v. wire,
 send a telegram
ipahayag /ee-puh-high-AHG/
 v. declare, announce
ipalabas /ee-puh-lah-BAHS/
 v. stage, produce
ipaliwanag /ee-pahl-ee-WAH-
 nahg/ v. explain
ipanaginip /ee-pahn-uh-
 GEE-nihp/ v. dream
ipasok /ee-PAH-sohk/ v.
 enter
ipinid /ee-peen-IHD/ v.
 close
ipit /EE-piht/ n. pinch
ipitin /ee-PEET-ihn/ v.
 pinch, apply pressure

iraos /ee-RAH-ohs/ v. take
place, get along

isa /ee-SAH/ num. one

isabit /ee-SAH-biht/ v.
hook

isaksak /ee-sahk-SAHK/ v.
cram, stuff, jam into

isaktan /ee-sahk-TAHN/ v.
hurt, injure

isahan /ee-SAH-hahn/ n.
unit; adv. singly

isahog /ee-sah-HOHG/ v.
season, add seasoning

isampay /ee-sahm-PIE/ v.
hang (laundry)

isang /ee-SAHNG/ art. a,
an, one

isara /ee-sahr-AH/ v. close

isarhan /ee-sahr-HAHN/ v.
shut down, close

isauli /ee-sah-oo-LIH/ v.
give back, return

isda /ees-DAH/ n. fish

isip /EE-sihp/ n. thought

isipin /ee-SEEP-ihn/ v.
think

istante /ees-TAHN-tih/ n.
 shelf
isukat /ee-SOO-kaht/ v.
 fit, try on
isupot /ee-SOO-poht/ v.
 bag, sack
itaas /ee-tuh-AHS/ adv.
 upstairs, above, aloft
itaboy /ee-tah-BOY/ v.
 ward off, fend off
itago /ee-TAH-goh/ v. keep,
 put away for safekeeping
itala /ee-TAHL-ah/ v.
 record
itambal /ee-TAHM-bahl/ v.
 team up, team with
itapal /ee-TAH-pahl/ v.
 affix, stick to, apply
iti /EE-tih/ n. dysentery
itik /EE-tihk/ n. duck
itim /ee-TEEM/ n. black
itimin /ee-tihm-IHN/ v.
 blacken
itlog /iht-LOHG/ n. egg
ito /ee-TOH/ prn. this, it
itudla /ee-tood-LAH/ v. aim

itulak /ee-TOO-lahk/ v.
push, shove
ituloy /ee-too-LOOY/ v.
continue, proceed
ituro /ee-TOOR-oh/ v. di-
rect, point, teach
iulat /ee-OO-laht/ v. re-
port
iyak /ee-YAHK/ n. cry, sob
iyakan /ee-yahk-AHN/ v. cry
iyan /ee-YAHN/ adj., prn.
that
iyo /ee-YOH/ adj. yours
iyon /ee-YOHN/ adj. that
one, that's the one
laba /luh-BAH/ v. launder,
wash clothes
labada /luh-BAH-dah/ n.
laundry
labaha /luh-BAH-hah/ n.
razor
labahan /lah-BAH-hahn/ n.
washing machine
laban /LAH-bahn/ n. fight;
prep. against

labanan /lah-bah-NAHN/ v.
fight, oppose
labas /lah-BAHS/ n. outside;
adv. outside
labasan /lah-BAHS-ahn/ n.
exit, outlet
labhan /lahb-HAHN/ v. wash
labi /LAH-bee/ n. lip
labimpito /lah-beem-pee-
TOH/ num. seventeen
labindalawa /lah-behn-dah-
luh-WAH/ num. twelve
labing-anim /lah-beeng-AHN-
eem/ num. sixteen
labing-apat /lah-beeng-AH-
paht/ num. fourteen
labing-isa /lah-beeng-ee-
SAH/ num. eleven
labingwalo /lah-beeng-wah-
LOH/ num. eighteen
labing-lima /lah-beeng-lee-
MAH/ num. fifteen
labinsiyam /lah-bihn-she-
AHM/ num. nineteen
labintatlo /lah-bihn-taht-
LOH/ num. thirteen

labis /LAH-bihs/ adj. ex-
tra, excessive
labnawin /lahb-nahw-IHN/ v.
dilute
lakad /LAH-kahd/ n. walk
lakarin /lah-KAHR-ihn/ v.
walk
lakas /lah-KAHS/ n. strength
lakasan ang loob /lah-kahs-
AHN ahng loh-OHB/ adv.
boldly, courageously
lakbayin /lahk-buy-IHN/ v.
travel, journey
laki /lahk-EE/ n. size
lakihan /lahk-EE-hahn/ v.
enlarge
lakipan /lah-kee-PAHN/ v.
contain
laktaw /lahk-TAHW/ n. skip,
omission
laktawan /lahk-TAHW-ahn/ v.
skip, omit
lagari /lah-GAHR-ee/ n. saw
lagariin /lah-gahr-EE-
ihn/ v. saw, shuttle
lagi /LAHG-ih/ adv. always

lagnat /lahg-NAHT/ n. fever
lahad /LAH-hahd/ n. statement, narration
lahat /lah-HAHT/ adj., prn.
all
lahatan /lah-HAHT-ahn/ adj.
general
lahi /LAH-hee/ n. race,
background
lahok /lah-HOHK/ n. in-
gredient, element
lalaki /lah-LAH-kee/ n. man
lalaking kapatid /lah-LAH-
keeng kah-puh-TIHD/ n.
brother
lalagyan /lah-lug-YAHN/ n.
vessel, container
lalamunan /lah-luh-MOON-
ahn/ n. throat
lalangin /lah-lahng-IHN/ v.
create
lalawigan /lah-lah-WEEG-ahn/
n. province
lalim /LAH-leem/ n. depth
laliman /lah-LEE-mahn/ v.
deepen

lalo /LAH-loh/ adv. more,
moreso, more especially

lamad /LAH-mahd/ n. mem-
brane, gristle

laman /lah-MAHN/ n. con-
tents, flesh portion

lamang /LAH-mahng/ adv.
only

lamang /luh-MAHNG/ n. ad-
vantage

lamangan /lah-mahng-AHN/ v.
exploit, take advantage of

lamas /lah-MAHS/ n. mess,
muss, crumple

lamasin /lah-MAHS-ihn/ v.
muss, crumple

lamat /LAH-maht/ n. crack

lamatan /lah-MAHT-ahn/ v.
crack

lamay /LAH-my/ n. night
work, vigil

lamayin /lah-MY-ihn/ v.
moonlight, work overtime

lambat /lahm-BAHT/ n. net

lamok /lah-MOHK/ n. mos-
quito

lampahin /lahm-pah-HIHN/ v.
 weaken
lampas /lahm-PAHS/ adv. excessive, exceeded, beyond
lana /LAHN-ah/ n. wool
landas /lahn-DAHS/ n. path,
 trail
landasin /lahn-dahs-IHN/ v.
 trail, back-track
lang /lahng/ adv. only
langaw /LAHNG-ahw/ n. fly
langis /lahng-EHS/ n. oil
langisan /lahng-ehs-AHN/ v.
 lubricate, oil
langit /LAHNG-iht/ n. sky,
 heaven
langoy /lahng-OY/ v. swim
languyan /LAHNG-oo-yahn/
 n. swim, swimming event
lanilya /lah-NEEL-yah/
 adj. woolen
lansihin /lahn-see-HIHN/
 v. trick, deceive
lanta /lahn-TAH/ adj.
 wilted

lantad /lahn-TAHD/ adj. in
 plain view, exposed
lantay /lahn-TIE/ adj. pure
laot /lah-OHT/ n. midst
lapad /LAH-pahd/ n. width
lapit /LAH-piht/ n. near-
 ness, proximity
lapitan /lah-PEE-tahn/ v.
 near, approach
larawan /luh-RAHW-ahn/ n.
 picture, image
laruan /lah-ROO-ahn/ n. toy
laruin /lah-roo-IHN/ v. play
lasa /LAHS-uh/ n. taste,
 flavor
lasapin /lah-sahp-IHN/ v.
 taste, experience
lasing /lah-SIHNG/ adj. in-
 toxicated, drunk
lasingan /LAHS-eeng-ahn/ n.
 bar, drinking establishment
lason /LAHS-ohn/ n. poison
lasunin /lah-SOON-ihn/ v.
 poison
lata /LAHT-ah/ n. tin can

latak /LAH-tahk/ n. residue
latag /LAH-tahg/ v. spread
lawa /LAH-wah/ n. lake
lawak /LAH-wahk/ n. area,
  extent
lawitan /lah-wiht-AHN/ v.
  favor, give attention to
laya /LIE-uh/ adj. free
layag /LIE-ahg/ n. sail
layas /LIE-ahs/ v. wander,
  roam
layo /LIE-oh/ n. distance
layon /LIE-ohn/ n. aim
libabo /lee-BAH-boh/ n.
  sink
liban /LEE-bahn/ prep. except; v. postpone
libangan /lee-BAHNG-ahn/ n.
  pleasure, amusement
libangin /lee-bahng-IHN/
  v. amuse
libingan /lee-BEENG-ahn/
  n. cemetary
libis /lee-BIHS/ n. slope
libo /LEE-boh/ num. thousand

libutin /lee-BOOT-ihn/ v.
tour, get around
likas /lee-KAHS/ adj. in-
born, natural
likha /leek-HAH/ v. create
liko /lee-KOH/ v. turn
likod /lee-KOHD/ n. back
liksihan /lihk-see-HAHN/ v.
speed
ligalig /lee-GAHL-ihg/ n.
trouble
ligaligin /lee-gah-LEEG-
ihn/ v. trouble, make
trouble
ligawan /lee-GAHW-ahn/ v.
date, court, call on
ligiran /lee-GIHR-ahn/ v.
surround
ligo /LEE-goh/ n. bath
ligta /lihg-TAH/ v. omit
ligtas /lihg-TAHS/ v. save,
rescue; adj. safe
liham /LEE-hahm/ n. letter
lihi /lee-HEE/ n. concep-
tion; v. conceive (birth)

lihim /LEE-heem/ n. secret
lihimin /lee-HIHM-ihn/ v.
 plot, conspire
lihis /lih-HIHS/ v. detour
liig /lih-EHG/ n. neck
lila /LEE-luh/ adj. violet
lilim /LEE-leem/ n. shade
liliman /lee-LEE-mahn/ v.
 shade, place a shade
lilip /LEE-lihp/ n. hem-
 stitch; v. stitch
lima /lee-MAH/ num. five
limampu /lee-mahm-POH/
 num. fifty
limbag /lihm-BAHG/ n. print
limbagin /lihm-bahg-IHN/
 v. print, publish
limos /lee-MOHS/ n. alms,
 charity; v. give to the
 poor
limpak /lihm-PAHK/ n. lump
limutin /lee-MOO-tihn/ v.
 forget
lingkod /leeng-KOHD/ n.
 service

linggo /leeng-GOH/ n. week
Linggo /Leeng-GOH/ n. Sunday
lingguhan /leeng-GOO-hahn/
  adj. weekly
linggu-linggo /leeng-GOO
  leeng-GOH/ adv. weekly,
  every week
linisin /lee-NEES-ihn/ v.
  clean
liparin /lee-pahr-IHN/ v.
  fly
lipunan /lee-POO-nahn/ n.
  society
listahan /lihs-TAH-hahn/
  n. list
lisyain /lihs-yah-IHN/ v.
  err, mistake
litrato /lee-TRAH-toh/ n.
  photograph, picture
liwasan /LEE-wahs-ahn/ n.
  park
liyabe /lee-YAH-bay/ n.
  wrench
lobo /LOH-boh/ n. balloon
lokohin /loh-KOH-hihn/ v.
  fool, trick, deceive

loob /loh-OHB/ n. interior
loro /LOH-roh/ n. parrot
lubak /loo-BAHK/ n. rut,
 pothole
lubid /LOO-bihd/ n. rope
lukbutan /luhk-BOOT-ahn/
 n. pocket
lukso /luhk-SOH/ n. jump
luksuhin /luhk-soo-HIHN/
 v. hurdle, vault
lugar /loo-GAHR/ n. place
luha /LOO-huh/ n. tears
luhog /LOO-hohg/ n. re-
 quest, entreaty
lulunin /loo-loon-IHN/ v.
 swallow
luma /LOO-mah/ adj. old,
 outdated, obsolete
lumaban /loo-MAH-bahn/ v.
 fight, resist
lumala /loo-mah-LAH/ v.
 worsen, deteriorate
lumapit /loo-MAHP-iht/ v.
 approach, near
lumbay /loom-BY/ n. sorrow

lumitaw /loom-ee-TAHW/ v.
  appear, show up
lumukso /loo-mook-SOH/ v.
  leap, bound
lumuhod /loo-moo-HOHD/ v.
  kneel
lumulan /loo-MOO-lahn/ v.
  ride
lundagin /loon-dahg-IHN/
  v. jump, spring
Lunes /Loo-nehs/ n. Monday
lungga /loong-GAH/ n. den,
  burrow
lunggati /loong-GAH-tee/
  n. wish, desire, longing
lunsad /loon-SAHD/ n. pier
lunsod /loon-SOHD/ n. city
luntian /loon-TEE-ahn/
  adj. green
lunurin /loo-NOO-rihn/ v.
  drown
lupa /LOO-pah/ n. earth,
  soil, land, ground
lupi /loo-PIH/ n. fold
lupigin /loo-PIHG-ihn/ v.
  conquer, vanquish

lupon /LOO-pohn/ n.
committee
luraan /loor-ah-AHN/ v.
spit
lusawin /loo-SAHW-ihn/ v.
melt, dissolve
lusubin /loo-SOOB-ihn/ v.
attack
lusutan /loo-soo-TAHN/ v.
slip, pass through
lutasin /loo-tahs-IHN/ v.
solve, settle
lutuin /loo-TOO-ihn/ v.
cook
luwagan /loo-wahg-AHN/ v.
loosen, make room
luwal /loo-WAHL/ v. emit,
produce
luwalhati /loo-wahl-HAH-
tee/ n. glory
luwalhatiin /loo-wahl-hah-
TEE-ihn/ v. glorify
luya /LOO-yah/ n. ginger
maaari /mah-ah-AHR-ee/
adj. possible; v. can

maaga /muh-AH-gah/ adj.,
 adv. early
maagap /muh-AHG-ahp/ adj.
 prompt
maalat /mah-AH-laht/ adj.
 salty
maalingasaw /muh-ah-leeng-
 AH-sahw/ adj. putrid
maalinsangan /muh-ah-leen-
 SAHNG-ahn/ adj. hot, humid
maamo /mah-AHM-oh/ adj.
 tame, compliant
maasa /mah-AHS-ah/ adj.
 hopeful
maasim /mah-AHS-eem/ adj.
 sour
mababa /muh-BAH-bah/ adj.
 low, short
mababaw /muh-BAH-bahw/
 adj. shallow
mabagal /muh-BAHG-ahl/
 adj. slow, reluctant
mabagsik /mah-bahg-SIHK/
 adj. fierce, ferocious
mabait /mah-by-EHT/ adj.
 kind, innocuous, virtuous

mabangis /mah-bahng-IHS/
 adj. wild
mabango /mah-bahng-OH/ adj.
 fragrant, aromatic
mabigat /mah-bee-GAHT/ adj.
 heavy
mabilis /mah-bee-LIHS/ adj.
 fast, rapid, speedy
mabilog /mah-BEE-lohg/ adj.
 round, circular
mabini /mah-BEE-nee/ adj.
 gentle
mabisa /mah-BEE-sah/ adj.
 effective
mabuo /mah-boo-OH/ adj.
 entire; adv. entirely
mabusog /mah-boo-SOHG/ adj.
 full, satiated (food)
mabuti /mah-BOOT-ee/ adj.
 good
makaaabala /mah-kuh-ah-ah-
 BAHL-uh/ v. inconvenience
makabago /mah-kuh-BAH-goh/
 adj. modern, up-to-date
makalakuti /mah-kah-luh-
 koo-TEE/ adj. fancy

makalawa /mah-KAH-lah-WAH/
  adv. twice removed, day
  after tomorrow
makapal /mah-kuh-PAHL/
  adj. thick
makasalanan /mah-kahs-ah-
  LAH-nahn/ adj. guilty
makata /mah-KAH-tah/ n.
  poet
makinig /mah-keen-IHG/ v.
  listen, hear
makinis /mah-KEEN-ihs/
  adj. smooth
makipot /mah-KEE-poht/
  adj. narrow, tight
makirot /mah-kee-ROHT/
  adj. sore, painful
makislap /mah-kees-LAHP/
  adj. bright, shiny
makulot /mah-koo-LOHT/
  adj. curly, wavy
makunat /mah-KOO-naht/
  adj. tough, gritty
madalas /mah-duh-LAHS/ adv.
  often; adj. frequent

madali /mah-duh-LEE/ adj.
 easy, quick
madasalin /mah-dah-SAHL-
 ihn/ adj. religious
madilim /mah-dee-LEEM/
 adj. dark, murky
madla /mahd-LAH/ n. public
madusa /mah-DOO-sah/ adj.
 wretched, suffering
magaan /mah-guh-AHN/ adj.
 light, easy to bear
magalas /mahg-uh-LAHS/
 adj. coarse, rough
magaling /mahg-uh-LIHNG/
 adj. excellent
maganak /mahg-AH-nahk/ n.
 family
maganda /mah-gahn-DAH/
 adj. beautiful
magaral /mahg-AH-rahl/ v.
 study
magaslaw /mah-gahs-LAHW/
 adj. crude, vulgar
magbakasakali /mahg-bah-
 kuh-suh-KAH-lee/ v. chance

magbiro /mahg-beer-OH/ v.
  joke, jest, kid
magkakapitbahay /mahg-kah-
  kah-peet-BAH-high/ n.
  neighborhood
magkakilala /mahg-kah-kee-
  LAH-lah/ adj. familiar,
  acquainted
magkapareho /mahg-kah-pahr-
  AY-hoh/ adj. alike
magkasabay /mahg-kah-suh-
  BUY/ adv. together, in
  unison
magkita /mahg-KEE-tuh/ v.
  see
maghilom /mahg-HEE-lohm/
  v. heal, cure
maghintay /mahg-heen-TIE/
  v. wait
maginaw /mah-geen-AHW/
  adj. cold
maging /mahg-EENG/ v.
  become
magingat /mahg-EENG-aht/ v.
  be careful, take care

maginhawa /mah-geen-HAHW-ah/ adj. convenient, comfortable

maginoo /mah-geen-OH-oh/ n. gentleman; adj. gentlemanly

magipon /mahg-EE-pohn/ v. collect, save

maglakip /mahg-LAH-kehp/ v. enclose, include

maglaro /mahg-lahr-OH/ v. play

maglibot /mahg-lee-BOHT/ tour

maglinis /mahg-LEE-nees/ v. clean

magmalasakit /mahg-mahl-ah-SAHK-iht/ v. care

magmaneho /mahg-mah-NAY-hoh/ v. drive (vehicle)

magnanakaw /mahg-nah-NAH-kahw/ n. thief

magpabuya /mahg-pah-BOO-yah/ v. tip, leave a tip

magpakabusog /mahg-pah-kuh-boo-SOHG/ v. feast, eat up

magpalamig /mahg-pah-luh-
  MEHG/ v. refresh oneself
magparangal /mahg-pahr-ahng-
  AHL/ v. host, fete
magpasaya /mahg-pah-sigh-
  AH/ v. enjoy oneself
magpasimuno /mahg-pah-see-
  MOO-noh/ v. lead
magsabi /mahg-SAH-bee/ v.
  say, voice
magsasaka /mahg-sah-SAHK-
  uh/ n. farmer
magsisi /mahg-SEE-see/ v.
  regret
magsumbong /mahg-soom-
  BOONG/ v. complain
magtrabaho /mahg-truh-
  BAH-hoh/ v. work
magulang /mah-GOO-lahng/
  n. parent
magusap /mahg-OO-sahp/ v.
  talk, discuss
mahaba /mah-HAH-bah/ adj.
  long
mahal /muh-HAHL/ adj. dear,
  expensive

mahalaga /mah-hahl-uh-GAH/
  adj. valuable, important
maharlika /mah-hahr-LEE-
  kah/ adj. noble
mahigpit /mah-heeg-PIHT/
  adj. tight, strict
mahilig /mah-HEEL-ihg/ adj.
  willing, interested
mahina /mah-HEE-nah/ adj.
  weak
mahinala /mah-hee-NAHL-ah/
  adj. suspect, suspicious
mahinhin /mah-heen-HIHN/
  adj. polite, courteous
mahirap /mah-HEER-ahp/
  adj. difficult
mahusay /mah-HOO-sigh/
  adj. skillful, adept
maikli /mah-ihk-LIH/ adj.
  short
maigsi /mah-ihg-SEE/ adj.
  short
mainam /mah-EE-nahm/ adj.
  pleasant, nice
maingat /mah-IHNG-aht/
  adj. careful, cautious

maingay /mah-IHNG-igh/ adj.
 loud, noisy
mainggitin /mah-eeng-GIHT-
 een/ adj. envious
mainit /mah-EEN-iht/ adj.
 warm
maisip /mah-EE-sihp/ adj.
 thoughtful
maitim /mah-ee-TEEM/ adj.
 black
malabo /mah-LAH-boh/ adj.
 vague, imprecise
malakas /mahl-ah-KAHS/ adj.
 powerful, influential
malaki /mah-lah-KAY/ adj.
 big, large
malagkit /mah-lahg-KIHT/
 adj. sticky, waxy
malalim /mah-LAH-leem/
 adj. deep
malamang /mahl-ah-MAHNG/
 adv. probably
malambing /mah-lahm-
 BIHNG/ adj. affectionate
malambot /mah-lahm-BOHT/
 adj. soft

malamig /mah-luh-MIHG/
 adj. cold
malantik /mah-lahn-TIHK/
 adj. curved, graceful
malapad /mah-LAH-pahd/ adj.
 wide
malapit /mah-LAH-piht/ adj.
 close, near
malapit na /mah-lah-piht
 NAH/ adv. soon
malas /MAHL-ahs/ adj. bad,
 evil, unlucky
malasakit /mahl-uh-SAHK-
 iht/ n. concern
malawak /mah-LAHW-ahk/ adj.
 grand, great, majestic
malayo /muh-LIE-oh/ adj.
 far, distant
mali /mah-LEE/ adj. wrong,
 incorrect, mistaken
maliksi /mah-lihk-SEE/
 adj. quick, agile
maligaya /mahl-ee-GUY-uh/
 adj. happy
maligo /mah-LEE-goh/ v.
 bathe, shower

malihim /mah-LEE-heem/ adj.
  secretive, secret
maliit /mah-lee-IHT/ adj.
  little, small
malinaw /mah-LEE-nahw/ adj.
  clear
malinis /mah-LEE-nihs/ adj.
  clean
maliwanag /mah-lee-WAHN-
  ahg/ adj. clear
malubha /mah-loob-HAH/ adj.
  serious, critical, grave
malungkot /mah-loong-KOHT/
  adj. sad
malupit /mah-loo-PIHT/ adj.
  cruel
malusog /mah-loo-SOHG/ adj.
  healthy
maluwag /mah-loo-WAHG/ adj.
  broad, spacious, roomy
maluwang /mah-loo-WAHNG/
  adj. loose
mama /MAHM-ah/ n. fellow
mamamayan /mah-mah-MY-ahn/
  n. citizen, resident

mamaya /mah-mah-YAH/ adv.
 later, after a while
mamayang gabi /mah-mah-
 YAHNG guh-BEE/ adv.
 tonight
mamili /mah-MEE-lee/ v.
 pick, choose, select
mamili /mah-mee-LIH/ v.
 shop, purchase
mamuhay /mah-MOO-high/ v.
 live, exist
man /mahn/ adv. though, on
 the other hand
manananggol /mahn-ah-nahng-
 GOHL/ n. lawyer, attorney
mananayaw /mahn-ah-NIGH-
 ahw/ n. dancer
mananghali /mahn-ahng-HAH-
 lee/ v. lunch, have lunch
manatili /mahn-uh-TEE-lee/
 v. stay, remain
mandaraya /mahn-duh-RYE-
 ah/ n. cheat, swindler
mang /mahng/ ref. Mr.,
 master, "uncle" (as
 humorous usage)

mangagawa /mahn-gah-GAHW-ah/ n. worker, laborer

mangangalakal /mah-ngah-ngah-LAH-kahl/ n. trader

mangangatay /mah-ngah-NGAH-tie/ n. butcher

mangasiwa /mahng-ah-SEE-wuh/ v. manage, administer

mangatuwiran /mahng-aht-WEER-ahn/ v. reason

mangkok /mahng-KOHK/ n. bowl

manggagamot /mahn-gah-GAH-moht/ n. doctor, physician

manghawa /mahng-HAHW-ah/ v. infect

mangugupit /mahn-goo-goo-PIHT/ n. barber

mangyari /mahng-YAHR-ee/ v. happen; conj. because

maniwala /mahn-ee-WAHL-uh/ v. believe, trust

manlalaro /mahn-lah-LAHR-oh/ n. player

manmanan /mahn-mahn-AHN/ v. spy on, snoop, nose into

manok /mahn-OHK/ n. chicken
manood /mahn-oo-OOD/ v.
  watch, view
mansanas /mahn-SAHN-ahs/
  n. apple
mantekilya /mahn-teh-KEEL-
  yah/ n. butter
mantika /mahn-TEE-kah/ n.
  grease, cooking oil
mantsa /mahnt-SAH/ n. stain
manunulat /mah-noo-NOO-
  laht/ n. writer
mapakinabang /mah-pahk-ee-
  NAH-bahng/ adj. useful,
  beneficial, advantageous
mapagbigay /mah-pahg-bee-
  GUY/ adj. generous
mapagkaibigan /mah-pahg-
  kah-ee-BEE-gahn/ adj.
  friendly
mapagmataas /mah-pahg-mah-
  tah-AHS/ adj. proud
mapahiya /mah-puh-HEE-
  yah/ v. embarrass
mapanganib /mah-pahng-AHN-
  eeb/ adj. dangerous

mapait /mah-pah-EHT/ adj.
 bitter
mapalad /mah-PAHL-ahd/ adj.
 fortunate, favorable
mapula /mah-poo-LAH/ adj.
 red
mapurol /mah-poo-ROHL/ adj.
 dull
maputi /mah-poo-TEE/ adj.
 white
maputla /mah-poot-LAH/ adj.
 pale, pallid
marahil /mah-RAH-heel/ adv.
 perhaps
marami /mah-RAH-mee/ adj.,
 adv. much, many
maramot /mah-RAH-moht/
 adj. selfish
marikit /mah-ree-KIHT/
 adj. pretty
Marso /MAHR-soh/ n. March
Martes /Mahr-TEHS/ n.
 Tuesday
martilyo /mahr-TEEL-yoh/
 n. hammer

marumi /mah-roo-MEE/ adj.
  dirty
marunong /mah-ROON-ohng/
  adj. smart, clever
marupok /mah-roo-POHK/ adj.
  fragile
masakit /mah-sah-KEHT/ adj.
  painful
masaklap /mah-sahk-LAHP/
  adj. unpleasant
masahol /mah-SAH-hohl/ adj.
  worse
masama /mah-sah-MAH/ adj.
  bad
masaya /mah-sah-YAH/ adj.
  merry, cheerful, gay
maski /mahs-KEE/ conj.
  although, despite
maski na /mahs-kee NAH/
  adv. regardless, anyway
masdan /mahs-DAHN/ v.
  observe
maselang /mah-SAY-lahng/
  adj. particular, fastidious

masinop /mah-SEEN-ohp/ adj.
 practical
masipag /mah-SEE-pahg/ adj.
 active, industrious
masungit /mah-SOONG-iht/
 adj. sullen, cross
masunurin /mah-soo-NOOR-
 ihn/ adj. obedient
masuwerte /mah-SWEHR-tay/
 adj. lucky, fortunate
mata /maht-AH/ n. eye
mataas /mah-tah-AHS/ adj.
 high
mataba /mah-tah-BAH/ adj.
 fat
matabang /mah-tah-BAHNG/
 adj. mild, bland, tepid
matagal /maht-ah-GAHL/
 adj. tedious, long
matahin /mah-tah-HIHN/ v.
 scorn, look down on
matalab /maht-ah-LAHB/
 adj. efficient
matalas /mah-TAHL-ahs/
 adj. sharp

matalim /mah-tah-LEEM/ adj.
 sharp, pointed
matalino /maht-ah-LEE-noh/
 adj. wise, intelligent
matamis /maht-ah-MEES/ adj.
 sweet
matanda /mah-tahn-DAH/
 adj. old
matangkad /mah-tahng-KAHD/
 adj. tall
matapang /mah-TAH-pahng/
 adj. combative, plucky
matapat /mah-tah-PAHT/ adj.
 forthright, truthful
matatag /mah-tah-TAHG/ adj.
 stout, firm, solid
matay /mah-TIE/ v. die
matibay /mah-TEE-by/ adj.
 durable
matigas /maht-ee-GAHS/
 adj. hard, stiff
matindi /mah-tihn-DEE/ adj.
 solemn, serious
matino /maht-ee-NOH/ adj.
 sensible

matira /MAHT-eer-uh/ v. remain, be left over, last

matiyaga /muh-tee-uh-GAH/ adj. persistent, persevering

matulungin /MAH-too-loong-IHN/ adj. helpful

matunton /MAH-toon-tohn/ v. track, trace

matutuhan /mah-too-TOO-hahn/ v. learn

matuwa /mah-too-AH/ v. be glad, rejoice

matwid /maht-WIHD/ adj. straight, direct

maupo /mah-oo-POH/ v. sit

mausisa /mah-oo-SEE-sah/ adj. curious, inquisitive

mawala /mah-wah-LAH/ v. disappear

may /may/ v. there is, there are

may-ari /may AHR-ee/ n. owner

may gagawin /may gah-guh-WEEN/ adj. busy, occupied

may sakit /may sah-KEHT/
 adj. sick, ill
mayroon /may-oh-OON/ v.
 have
mayumi /mah-yoo-MEE/ adj.
 modest
mga /muh-NGAH/ part. indicating plurality; adv.
 approximately, roughly
minsan /MIHN-sahn/ adv.
 occasionally
Miyerkoles /Mee-YEHR-koh-
 lees/ n. Wednesday
mauna /mah-OO-nuh/ adv.
 first, forward, ahead
mayaman /mah-YAH-mahn/
 adj. wealthy, rich
Mayo /MY-oh/ n. May
medyo /MEHD-yoh/ adv. ra-
 ther, somewhat, fairly
mukha /mook-HAH/ n. face
mula /moo-LAH/ adv. since;
 prep. from, from the time
muli /moo-LEE/ adv. again
multa /mool-TAH/ n. fine,
 penalty

multo /mool-TOH/ n. ghost
mungkahi /moong-KAH-hee/ n.
  suggestion, motion
munti /moon-TEE/ adv. al-
  most, nearly
munukala /moon-oo-KAHL-ah/
  n. plan
mura /MOO-ruh/ adj. cheap,
  inexpensive
murahin /moo-RAH-hihn/ v.
  insult
musmos /moos-MOOS/ adj. in-
  experienced, innocent
mutya /moot-YAH/ n. pearl
muwang /moo-WAHNG/ n.
  common sense
na /nah/ conj. that, which;
  adv. already
nabakbak /nah-bahk-BAHK/ v.
  wear off, flake off
nabigo /nah-bee-GOH/ adj.
  disappointed
nabubuhay /nah-boo-BOO-
  high/ adj. alive, living
nakakalat /nah-kah-KAHL-
  aht/ adj. widespread

nakakatiis /nah-kah-kah-
tee-IHS/ v. endure, abide
nakahilera /nah-kuh-hee-
LEHR-ah/ adv. headlong
nakaraan /nah-kah-rah-AHN/
n. past
nakasarili /nah-kuh-sah-
REE-lih/ adv. personally,
privately
nakatira /nahk-uh-TEER-uh/
v. dwell, reside, live
nakatulog /nahk-uh-TOO-
lohg/ v. sleep
nakatunganga /nahk-uh-too-
NGAH-ngah/ adj. vulnerable
nakawin /nah-KAHW-een/ v.
steal
nakilala /nah-kee-LAH-lah/
be introduced, get to
know, be acquainted
nagaalaala /nahg-ah-AHL-uh-
AHL-uh/ adj. wary
nagalinlangan /nahg-ahl-
een-LAHNG-ahn/ v. doubt
nagalit /nah-GAHL-iht/ adj.
angry, mad

nagiging /nah-gee-GEENG/ v.
  becoming
nagiisa /nahg-ee-ee-SAH/
  adj. alone; adv. by one's
  self
naging /nahg-EENG/ v.
  became
nagmamadali /nahg-MAH-mahd-
  uh-LEE/ adj. urgent, in a
  hurry
nagugutom /nah-goo-GOO-
  tohm/ adj. hungry
nahiya /nuh-HEE-yuh/ adj.
  ashamed, embarrassed
nahuli /nah-hoo-LEE/ adj.
  late
nainis /nah-een-IHS/ adj.
  upset, infuriated
naisin /nah-EES-ihn/ v.
  desire, want, wish
namnam /nahm-NAHM/ n. flavor
namukhaan /NAH-mook-huh-
  AHN/ v. recognize
namumulaklak /nah-MOO-moo-
  lahk-LAHK/ v. flower,
  blossum

nanalo /nah-NAHL-oh/ adj.
  victorious, successful
nang /nahng/ conj. when,
  whenever
nangasim /nahng-AHS-eem/
  v. sour, become sour
napaka /NAH-pah-kah/ adv.
  very
nasa /NAHS-ah/ prep. in
nasaan /nah-suh-AHN/ conj.
  from where, whence
nasisiyahan /nah-SEE-see-
  yuh-HAHN/ adj. content,
  satisfied
natakot /nuh-TAH-koht/
  adj. afraid
natin /NAHT-ihn/ adj. ours
natutulog /nah-too-TOO-
  lohg/ adj. asleep
natuwa /nah-too-AH/ adj.
  glad
nauhaw /nah-oo-HAHW/ adj.
  thirsty
negosyante /nee-gohs-YAHN-
  tay/ n. merchant

ng /nahng/ prep. of

nga /ngah/ adv. really; ex.
  please

ngaligkig /ngah-lihg-KIHG/
  v. tremble, shiver

ngangaral /ngah-NGAHR-ahl/
  v. preach, sermonize

ngawngaw /NGAHW-ngahw/ v.
  scold

ngayon /nigh-OON/ adv. now

ngayong araw /nigh-oon AHR-
  ahw/ n., adv. today

ngiki /NGEE-kih/ n. chills

ngilo /ngee-LOH/ v. wince

nginig /ngee-NIHG/ v.
  tremble, shake

ngipin /NGEE-pihn/ n. tooth

ngisay /ngee-SIGH/ v. con-
  tort, writhe, convulse

ngiti /ngee-TIH/ n. smile

ngitian /ngee-tee-AHN/ v.
  smile

nguni't /NGOO-niht/ conj.
  but

ngupas /ngoo-PAHS/ v. fade

ni /nee/ conj. neither, nor;
 prep. by, of
nilalabahan /nee-lah-lahb-
 AH-hahn/ n. wash, laundry
ningas /NIHNG-ahs/ n. flame
ninuno /nee-NOO-noh/ n.
 ancestor
niya /nee-YAH/ prn. his,
 hers
Nobyembre /Nohb-YEHM-bray/
 n. November
noong araw /noo-OHNG AHR-
 ahw/ adv. ago, some time
 ago
nubok /NOO-bohk/ v. spy on,
 peep
o /oh/ conj. or
Oktubre /Ohk-TOO-bray/ n.
 October
oo /OH-oh/ adv. yes
oras /OH-rahs/ n. hour
orasan /oh-RAHS-ahn/ v.
 time; n. clock
ospital /ohs-pee-TAHL/ n.
 hospital

otel /oh-TEHL/ n. hotel
pa /pah/ adv. yet, still,
 else
paa /puh-AH/ n. foot
paakyat /pah-ahk-YAHT/
 adj. vertical
paalala /pah-uh-LAH-lah/
 v. remind
paalam /pah-ah-LAHM/ n.
 good-bye
paandarin /PAH-ahn-dahr-
 IHN/ v. power, start up
paano /pah-AHN-oh/ int.
 how?
paaralan /PAH-ahr-ahl-AHN/
 n. school
paaralin /PAH-ahr-ahl-IHN/
 v. educate
pabango /pah-bahng-OH/ n.
 perfume
pabaya /puh-by-AH/ adj.
 careless, negligent
pabayaan /puh-by-ah-AHN/
 v. overlook, tolerate
pabo /PAH-boh/ n. turkey

pabuya /pah-BOO-yah/ n. tip
pakamahalin /pahk-ah-mah-
  hahl-IHN/ v. love
paki /pahk-EE/ part. indicating a request; ex. please!
pakialamin /PAHK-ee-ah-
  lahm-EEN/ v. interfere
pakikibaka /puh-KEE-kee-
  BAH-kuh/ n. struggle
pakikipagsapalaran /pah-KEE-
  kee-pahg-SAH-pahl-ahr-AHN/
  n. adventure
pakinabang /pah-keen-AH-
  bahng/ n. benefit, advantage, usefulness
pakintab /pah-kihn-TAHB/
  n. polish
pakintabin /PAH-kihn-tahb-
  IHN/ v. polish
pakislapin /PAH-kihs-lahp-
  IHN/ v. shine, make shiny
pako /PAH-koh/ n. nail
pakpak /pahk-PAHK/ n. wing
paksa /pahk-SAH/ n. topic
pakuan /pah-KOO-ahn/ v.
  nail, nail to

pakuluin /pah-koo-loo-IHN/
v. boil
pakundangan /pah-koon-
DAHNG-ahn/ n. respect,
consideration
pakundanganan /pah-koon-
dahng-AH-nahn/ v. respect,
show respect
pakuwan /pahk-WAHN/ n.
watermelon
pakyaw /pahk-YAHW/ n.
wholesale purchase
pakyawin /pahk-yahw-IHN/
v. buy wholesale
padala /puh-dahl-AH/ n.
shipment
padparin /pahd-pahr-IHN/ v.
scud, float along, drift
ashore
pagaari /pahg-ah-AHR-ih/
n. possession, property
pagabot /pahg-ah-BOHT/
n. reach
pagasa /pahg-AHS-ah/ n.
hope

pagbabago /pahg-bah-BAH-
 goh/ n. change
pagbalik /pahg-bah-LIHK/
 n. return
pagbawalan /PAHG-bah-wahl-
 ahn/ v. forbid, prohibit
pagkakakilala /pahg-KAH-
 kah-kee-lah-LAH/ n.
 recognition
pagkakakitaan /pahg-KAH-
 kah-kee-tah-AHN/ n.
 employment
pagkakataon /pahg-kah-KAH-
 tah-OHN/ n. opportunity
pagkatapos /pahg-kah-TAH-
 pohs/ adv. afterwards
pagkahatid /PAHG-kah-
 hah-TIHD/ n. delivery
pagkain /pahg-KAH-ihn/ n.
 food
pagkalinga /pahg-kah-
 LIHNG-ah/ n. care, pro-
 tection
pagkawala /PAHG-kah-wahl-
 AH/ n. disappearance
pagkit /pahg-KIHT/ n. wax

pagdaka /pahg-DAH-kah/ adv.
 immediately
pagdadahop /pahg-dah-dah-
 HOHP/ n. need, destitution
pagdating /pahg-dah-TIHNG/
 n. arrival
pagdiin /pahg-dee-IHN/ n.
 pressure
paghanga /pahg-HAHNG-ah/
 n. admiration
paghiwa-hiwalayin /pahg-hee-
 WAH hee-wah-lie-IHN/ v.
 sort, separate
paghiwalay /PAHG-hee-wah-
 LIE/ n. separation
pagibig /pahg-EE-bihg/ n.
 love
pagigihin /pahg-ee-GEE-
 hihn/ v. perfect, get it
 right
pagitan /pah-GEE-tahn/ n.
 interspace; prep. among,
 between
paglilibing /PAHG-lee-lee-
 BIHNG/ n. funeral

paglilitis /pahg-lee-LEE-tihs/ n. trial

pagod /pah-GOHD/ adj. tired

pagong /pah-GOHNG/ n. turtle

pagpagin /pahg-pahg-IHN/ v. wipe off, shake off

pagpalit /pahg-pahl-IHT/ n. exchange

pagpapaayos /PAHG-pah-pah-AHY-ohs/ n. repair

pagpapakilala /pahg-pah-pah-kee-LAH-lah/ n. formal introduction

pagpapahatid /PAHG-pah-pah-hah-TIHD/ n. express delivery

pagsama-samahin /pahg-suh-MAH suh-MAH-hihn/ v. mix together, pool

pagsasaka /pahg-sah-SAHK-ah/ n. cultivation, farming

pagsiyasat /pahg-see-YAHS-aht/ n. inquiry

pagsulit /pahg-SOO-liht/ n.
 examination
pagsulong /pahg-SOO-lohng/
 n. advance, trend
pagsusukat /PAHG-soo-soo-
 KAHT/ n. fitting, trying
 on (clothes)
pagtawag /pahg-TAHW-ahg/
 n. call
pagtiiisan /PAHG-tee-ees-
 AHN/ v. sacrifice
pagunlad /pahg-oon-LAHD/
 n. progress
pagurin /pah-GOOR-ihn/ v.
 tire
pagusapan /pahg-oo-SAHP-
 ahn/ n. discussion
pahatidkawad /pah-hah-TEED-
 KAH-wahd/ n. telegraph
pahayagan /PAH-high-uh-
 GAHN/ n. newspaper
pahinga /pah-hihng-AH/ n.
 rest, respite
pahingahin /pah-hihng-ah-
 HIHN/ v. rest

pahingi /pah-hihng-EE/ ex.
  let me borrow, let me use
pahintulot /pah-hihn-TOO-
  loht/ n. permission
pahintulutan /pah-hihn-too-
  LOO-tahn/ v. permit
pahiram /pah-heer-AHM/ ex.
  let me borrow your
paimbabaw /PAH-eem-buh-
  BAHW/ adj. artificial
pala /PAHL-ah/ n. shovel
pala /pahl-AH/ ex. so!
palabas /pahl-ah-BAHS/ n.
  program
palabasin /PAHL-ah-bahs-
  EEN/ v. program, put on,
  carry out
palabok /pah-LAH-bohk/ n.
  spice
palaka /pahl-ah-KAH/ n.
  frog
palakad /pah-LAH-kahd/ n.
  regulation, policy
palakasan /pahl-ah-KAHS-
  ahn/ n. influence, payola

palakol /pahl-ah-KOHL/ n.
 ax
palakpak /pahl-ahk-PAHK/
 n. applause
palagay /pahl-ah-GUY/ n.
 opinion
palagi /pah-LAHG-ee/ adv.
 always, constantly
palahatian /PAHL-ah-hah-
 TEE-ahn/ n. division
palahudyatan /pahl-ah-
 huhd-YAHT-ahn/ n. signal
palaisdaan /pahl-ah-ees-
 DAH-ahn/ n. fish pond
palaman /pah-lah-MAHN/ n.
 contents
palambutin /PAH-lahm-boot-
 IHN/ v. soften, tenderize
palanggana /PAH-lahng-GAHN-
 ah/ n. basin
palantsahin /PAH-lahnt-
 sah-HIHN/ v. iron, press
 (clothes)
palapag /pahl-ah-PAHG/ n.
 level, floor, story

palaso /pah-LAHS-oh/ n.
 arrow
palatuntunan /pahl-ah-toon-
 TOON-ahn/ n. program
palayain /pah-lie-AH-ihn/
 v. free, set free
palayok /pahl-ah-YOHK/ n.
 pot
palda /PAHL-dah/ n. skirt
palengke /pah-LEHNG-kee/
 n. market
palikuran /pah-lee-KOOR-
 ahn/ n. restroom
paligo /pah-LEE-goh/ n. bath
paligsahan /pah-lihg-SAH-
 hahn/ n. competition,
 contest
paliguan /pah-lee-GOO-ahn/
 v. bathe
paliparan /pah-lee-PAHR-
 ahn/ n. airport
palit /pahl-IHT/ n. rate,
 exchange rate
paliwanag /pahl-ee-WAHN-
 ahg/ n. explanation

palo /PAHL-oh/ n. stroke,
 beat
paluin /pah-LOO-ihn/ v.
 paddle, beat, stroke
pamagat /pah-mah-GAHT/ n.
 title
pamahalaan /PAH-mah-hahl-
 AH-ahn/ n. government
pamahiin /pah-mah-HEE-ihn/
 n. superstition
pamangkin /pah-mahng-KEEN/
 n. nephew, niece
pamantasan /pah-mahn-TAHS-
 ahn/ n. university
pamantayan /pah-mahn-TIE-
 ahn/ n. standard
pamaypay /pah-my-PIE/ n.
 fan
pambabae /pahm-bah-bah-
 AY/ adj. female
pambihira /pahm-bee-HEER-
 ah/ adj. odd, extra-
 ordinary
paminsan-minsan /pah-MIHN-
 sahn MIHN-sahn/ adv. now
 and then, occasionally

paminta /pah-mihn-TAH/ n.
pepper
pampaganda /PAHM-pah-gahn-
DAH/ n. ornament, decora-
tion
pampang /pahm-PAHNG/ n.
shore
pampaputok /PAHM-pah-poo-
TOHK/ n. explosive
pampook /pahm-poo-OHK/ adj.
local
pamumulsa /PAH-moo-mool-
SAH/ v. pocket
pana /PAHN-ah/ n. bow (for
archery)
panaginip /pahn-ah-GEEN-
ihp/ n. dream
panahon /pah-nah-HOHN/ n.
time, weather, season
panain /pah-NAH-ihn/ v.
shoot
pananagutan /PAH-nahn-ah-
GOOT-ahn/ n. responsibility
pananampalataya /PAH-nah-
nahm-pahl-ah-TIE-ah/ n.
faith, religious belief

panarili /pahn-ah-REE-lee/
 adj. private
panauhin /pahn-ah-OO-hihn/
 n. visitor, guest
panay /pahn-IGH/ adj. continuous; adv. entirely,
 continuously
pangako /pahng-AH-koh/ n.
 promise
pangakuan /pahng-ah-KOO-
 ahn/ v. promise
pang-ahit /pahng-AH-hiht/
 n. razor
pangalan /pahng-AHL-ahn/ n.
 name
pangalawa /pahng-ahl-ah-
 WAH/ adj. second
pangalawit /pahng-ahl-ah-
 WIHT/ n. hook
pangamba /pahn-gahm-BAH/
 n. worry, fear
panganay /pahng-AH-nigh/
 adj. eldest
pangangalakal /PAH-ngah-
 ngah-LAHK-ahl/ n. com-
 merce, business

panganganak /PAH-ngah-ngah-
 NAHK/ n. birth
pangangasiwa /PAH-ngah-ngah-
 SEE-wah/ n. management
panganib /pahng-AH-neeb/ n.
 danger
pangaod /pahn-GAH-ohd/ n.
 oar
pangarap /pahng-AHR-ahp/
 n. ambition, aspiration
pangaraw /pahng-AH-rahw/
 adj. daily
pangkaraniwan /PAHNG-kahr-
 ahn-EE-wahn/ adj. common
pangkat /pahng-KAHT/ n.
 party, group
pangkulay /pahng-KOO-lie/
 n. coloring
pangisa /pahng-ee-SAH/
 adj. first
pangit /PAHNG-iht/ adj.
 ugly
pangulo /pahng-OO-loh/ n.
 president
pangyarihin /pahng-yahr-
 EE-hihn/ v. cause

pangyayari /pahng-yah-YAHR-
ee/ n. event, incident
panibago /pahn-ee-BAH-goh/
n. change
panibugho /pahn-ee-boog-
HOH/ n. jealousy
paniki /pahn-EE-kih/ n. bat
panimbang /pah-neem-BAHNG/
n. balance, sense of
balance
panis /pahn-EES/ adj.
spoiled (food)
panisin /pahn-ees-IHN/ v.
spoil (food)
panitikan /pah-NEET-ee-
kahn/ n. literature
paniwala /pahn-ee-WAHL-ah/
n. belief
paniwalaan /PAHN-ee-wahl-
AH-ahn/ v. believe
panlalaki /pahn-lah-LAHK-
ee/ adj. male
pansin /pahn-SIHN/ n. no-
tice, attention
pantay /pahn-TIE/ adj. level

pantayin /pahn-tie-IHN/ v.
 smoothe, even out, level
pantiyon /pahn-tee-YOHN/
 n. grave
pantog /pahn-TOOG/ n.
 bladder
panukala /pahn-oo-KAHL-ah/
 n. proposal
panungkulan /pah-noong-KOO-
 lahn/ n. profession
panyo /pahn-YOH/ n.
 handkerchief
papel /pah-PEHL/ n. paper
para /PAHR-ah/ conj. in
 order to; ex. Stop!
para hindi /PAHR-ah hihn-
 DIH/ conj. lest, in order
 not to
para sa /PAHR-ah SAH/
 prep. for, for the sake of
paraan /pahr-uh-AHN/ n.
 process, way, method
paramiin /pah-rah-MEE-ihn/
 v. multiply
parang /PAH-rahng/ conj.
 as if

pare /PAHR-ay/ n. priest;
 ref. buddy, fellow
paris /PAHR-ees/ n. pair
parisan /pahr-EES-ahn/ v.
 match
parusa /pah-ROOS-ah/ n.
 punishment
parusahin /PAH-roos-ah-
 HIHN/ v. punish
pasa /pahs-AH/ n. bruise
pasahod /pah-SAH-hohd/ n.
 salary
pasalamatin /PAH-sahl-ah-
 MAHT-ihn/ v. thank
Pasko /Pahs-KOH/ n.
 Christmas
pasimula /PAH-see-moo-LAH/
 n. beginning
pasimuno /pah-see-MOON-oh/
 n. leader
pasiya /pahs-ee-YAH/ n.
 decision
pasok kayo /PAHS-ohk kigh-
 YOH/ ex. enter, come in
pasukan /pahs-oo-KAHN/ n.
 entrance, doorway

pasuin /pahs-OO-ihn/ v.
 scald, burn
pasyal /pahs-YAHL/ n. trip,
 stroll, walk
patak /pah-TAHK/ n. drop
patakaran /PAH-tah-kahr-
 AHN/ n. regulation
patag /PAH-tahg/ adj.
 level, smooth
patawad /pah-TAHW-ahd/ n.
 pardon, forgiveness
patay /pah-TIE/ adj. dead
patayin /pah-TIE-ihn/ v.
 kill, turn off
patawarin /pah-tah-WAHR-
 ihn/ v. pardon, forgive
pati /pah-TEE/ adv. also,
 moreover
patibong /pah-tee-BOHNG/
 n. trap
patiwarik /PAH-tee-wahr-
 IHK/ adv. upside-down
patlang /paht-LAHNG/ n.
 interval, space
patnubay /paht-NOO-buy/ n.
 guide

patnubayin /paht-noo-BUY-
 ihn/ v. guide
patnugot /paht-NOO-goht/
 n. director
patumangga /PAH-too-mahng-
 GAH/ n. pause, respite
patunayan /pah-too-NIGH-
 ahn/ v. prove
paumanhin /PAH-oo-mahn-
 HIHN/ n. apology
pauna /PAH-oo-NAH/ n.
 warning
paunawa /pah-oo-NAHW-ah/
 n. notice
pawis /PAHW-ees/ n. sweat,
 perspiration
pawisan /pah-WEES-ahn/ v.
 sweat, perspire
payag /PIE-ahg/ v. agree
payat /pie-AHT/ adj. thin,
 slender, sleek
payo /PIE-oh/ n. advice
payong /PIE-ohng/ n.
 umbrella
payuhan /pie-YOO-hahn/ v.
 advise

Pebrero /Pehb-RARE-oh/ n.
 February
peklat /PEHK-laht/ n. scar
pelikula /peh-LIHK-oo-lah/
 n. movie, film
pera /PEHR-ah/ n. money
perdible /pehr-DEE-blay/
 n. safety pin
petsa /PEHT-sah/ n. date
pikit /pee-KIHT/ v. shut
 the eyes, close the eyes
pikon /pee-KOHN/ adj. hy-
 persensitive, touchy
pighati /pihg-hah-TEE/ n.
 grief, affliction
pigi /pee-GEE/ n. hip
pigilin /pee-GEEL-ihn/ v.
 stop, pause, detain
pigsa /pihg-SAH/ n. boil,
 carbuncle
pila /PEE-lah/ n. line,
 queue
pilak /PEE-lahk/ n. silver
pilay /pee-LIE/ adj. lame
pili /PEE-lih/ n. choice,
 pick, selection

piliin /pee-LEE-ihn/ v. select, pick, choose
piling /PEEL-ihng/ n. side
pilipitin /peel-ee-PEET-ihn/
v. twist, wring
pilitin /pee-LEET-ihn/ v.
force, insist
pinaalis /PEE-nah-ah-LIHS/
v. fire, dismiss (employee)
pinaka /peen-ah-KAH/ adv.
most, least
pinakilala /PEEN-ah-kee-LAH-
luh/ v. introduce (social)
pinakain /peen-ah-KAH-een/
v. feed, feed to
pinagaralan /pee-nahg-ahr-
AHL-ahn/ n. education, con-
clusions drawn from observation
pinagbilhan /PEE-nahg-bihl-
HAHN/ n. sales, sale
pinagmulan /PEE-nahg-moo-
LAHN/ n. origin, source
pinahiram /PEEN-ah-heer-
AHM/ v. lend

pinamigay /PEE-nuh-mee-GUY/
 v. give away, donate
pinamili /PEE-nah-mee-LIH/
 n. purchase
pinapalitan /PEEN-ah-pahl-
 ee-TAHN/ v. exchange
pinggan /pihng-GAHN/ n.
 plate
pinoy /pee-NOHY/ n., adj.
 Filipino
pinsan /PIHN-sahn/ n.
 cousin
pinto /pihn-TOH/ n. door
pintuan /pihn-TOO-ahn/ n.
 doorway
pintura /pihn-TOOR-ah/ n.
 paint
pinukol /peen-oo-KOHL/ v.
 stone, throw rocks
pirituhin /peer-ee-TOO-
 hihn/ v. fry (food)
pirma /peer-MAH/ n.
 signature
pirmahan /peer-mah-HAHN/
 v. sign

pito /pee-TOH/ num. seven
pitpitin /piht-piht-IHN/
v. pound, flatten
pitumpu /pee-toom-POH/ num.
seventy
plantsa /PLAHNT-sah/ n.
clothes iron
po /poh/ ref. sir, ma'am
pook /poo-OHK/ n. zone,
vicinity, district
Poon /Poo-OHN/ n. Lord Je-
sus Christ
poot /poo-OHT/ n. hatred,
fury
posporo /POHS-pohr-oh/ n.
match, match-stick
pukawin /poo-KAHW-ihn/ v.
wake up
pukpukin /pook-pook-IHN/
v. hammer
pugad /POO-gahd/ n. nest
puhunan /poo-HOO-nahn/ n.
capital, investment
puhunanin /poo-hoo-NAHN-
ihn/ v. invest, underwrite

pula /poo-LAH/ adj. red
pulaan /poo-LAH-ahn/ v. de-
 fame, slander, stain
pulbos /pool-BOHS/ n.
 powder
pulgas /pool-GAHS/ n. flea
pulo /poo-LOH/ n. island
pulong /POO-lohng/ n.
 meeting
pulso /pool-SOH/ n. wrist
pulubi /poo-LOO-bee/ n.
 beggar
pulupot /poo-LOOP-oht/ adj.
 twisted, coiled, wound
 around
pumalya /poo-mahl-YAH/
 adj. absent
pumarito /poo-mahr-EE-toh/
 v. come, come here
pumila /poo-MEEL-ah/ v.
 line up, queue
pumunta /poo-MOON-tah/ v.
 go
pumusta /poo-moos-TAH/ v.
 bet, risk, gamble

pumutok /poo-moo-TOHK/ v.
 explode, burst
punasan /poo-NAHS-ahn/ v.
 wipe
punitin /poo-NIHT-ihn/ v.
 tear, rip
puno /POO-noh/ n. tree
puno /poon-OH/ adj. full
punuin /poo-noo-IHN/ v.
 fill, fill up
puri /POOR-ee/ n. praise
purihin /poor-EE-hihn/ v.
 praise
pusa /POOS-ah/ n. cat
puso /POO-soh/ n. heart
puti /poo-TEE/ adj. white
putik /POO-tihk/ n. mud
putlain /poot-LAH-ihn/
 adj. pale
putulin /poo-TOOL-ihn/ v.
 cut, sever
puwang /poo-WAHNG/ n. gap
puwede /poo-WAY-day/ adv.
 possibly; adj. possible
raw /rahw/ adv. reportedly

repolyo /ree-POHL-yoh/ n.
  cabbage
resibo /ray-SEE-boh/ n.
  receipt, sales slip
riles /REE-lehs/ n. rail,
  railway
rilos /ray-LOHS/ n. watch,
  wristwatch
rin /rihn/ adv. too, also
sa /sah/ prep. at, to
saan /sah-AHN/ int. where?
saanman /sah-ahn-MAHN/ adv.
  wherever
sabad /sah-BAHD/ n.
  interruption
Sabado /SAHB-ah-doh/ n.
  Saturday
sabaw /sah-BAHW/ n. soup
sabik /sah-BEEK/ adj.
  eager
sabihin /sah-BEE-hihn/ v.
  say
sabon /sah-BOHN/ n. soap
sabunin /sah-boon-IHN/ v.
  soap
saka /sah-KAH/ adv. then,
  additionally, at that time

sakahin /sah-KAH-hihn/ v.
 farm, cultivate crops
sakali /sah-KAHL-ee/ conj.
 in case, in the event of
sakay /suh-KIGH/ n. trip,
 round, bout, ride
sakbit /sahk-BIHT/ n. strap
sakdal /sahk-DAHL/ adv.
 extremely, exceedingly
sakim /sah-KEEM/ adj.
 greedy
sakit /sah-KEHT/ n. hurt,
 sickness
saklolo /sahk-LOH-loh/ n.
 aid, assistance
sakong /SAHK-ohng/ n. heel
sakop /sah-KOHP/ n. rule,
 governance, jurisdiction
saksi /sahk-SEE/ n. witness
saktan /sahk-TAHN/ n. harm,
 injury, hurt
sakuna /sah-KOON-ah/ n.
 accident
sakupin /sah-KOOP-ihn/ v.
 rule, govern

sadya /sahd-YAH/ n. aim,
  purpose
sadyain /sahd-yah-IHN/ v.
  intend, do intentionally
sagabal /sah-GAH-bahl/ n.
  obstacle
saging /SAHG-eeng/ n.
  banana
saglit /sahg-LIHT/ n.
  second, instant
sagot /sah-GOHT/ n. answer
sagutin /sah-goot-IHN/ v.
  answer, reply
sahig /sah-HEHG/ n. floor
sahod /SAH-hohd/ n. salary
sahog /sah-HOHG/ n. cooking
  ingredient
sala /SAHL-ah/ n. living
  room
salakay /sah-LAH-kigh/ n.
  attack, assault
salakayin /sah-lah-kigh-
  IHN/ v. attack
salamat /sah-LAH-maht/ n.
  thanks; ex. thank you

salamin /sahl-ah-MEEN/ n.
 glass, mirror, glasses
salapi /sah-lah-PEE/ n.
 money
salarin /sah-lah-REEN/ n.
 criminal
salawal /sahl-ah-WAHL/ n.
 pants, underwear
salbahe /sahl-BAH-hay/ adj.
 wicked, evil
saligan /sahl-ee-GAHN/ n.
 basis, foundation
salinan /sah-LEE-nahn/ v.
 transcribe
salita /sahl-ee-TAH/ n.
 word
salitain /sahl-ee-TAH-ihn/
 v. speak
salitang kalye /sahl-EE-
 tahng KAHL-yay/ n. slang
salubungin /sahl-oo-BOONG-
 ihn/ v. greet, welcome
salunga /sah-LOONG-ah/
 adv. upwards
saluysoy /sah-LOOY-sohy/
 n. stream, brook

samakatuwid /sah-MAH-kah-
TWIHD/ conj. therefore
samahan /sah-MAH-hahn/ v.
accompany, go with
samahan /sahm-ah-HAHN/ n.
union, association, league
samantala /sah-mahn-TAHL-
ah/ conj. while, in the
meantime, meanwhile
samantalahin /SAH-mahn-tah-
lah-HIHN/ v. exploit, take
advantage of
sama-sama /SAHM-ah SAHM-ah/
adv. altogether
sama-samahin /sahm-AH sah-
MAH-hihn/ v. mix together
sambahin /sahm-bah-HIHN/ v.
worship
samid /sah-MIHD/ v. choke
sampalin /sahm-pahl-IHN/ v.
slap, spank
sampu /sahm-POO/ num. ten
sanayin /sah-NAHY-ihn/ v.
practice, train
sankatauhan /SAHN-kah-tah-
OO-hahn/ n. mankind

sandaan /sahn-duh-AHN/ num.
 one hundred
sandalan /sahn-dahl-AHN/ v.
 lean against, recline
sandali /sahn-dah-LEE/ n.
 moment, minute
sandali lang /sahn-dah-LEE
 lahng/ ex. just a minute
sandok /sahn-DOHK/ n.
 scoop, ladle
sandukin /sahn-dook-IHN/
 v. scoop, dip
sanga /sahng-AH/ n. branch
sangkap /sahng-KAHP/ n.
 substance, material
sanggol /sahng-GOHL/ n. baby
sanggunian /sahng-goo-NEE-
 ahn/ n. council, board
sanhi /sahn-HEE/ n. cause
sanla /sahn-LAH/ v. pawn;
 n. collateral
sansinukob /sahn-see-NOO-
 kohb/ n. universe
sansinukbin /SAHN-seen-ook-
 BIHN/ adj. universal

santauhan /sahn-tah-OO-hahn/ n. population

sapagka't /sah-pahg-KAHT/ conj. because

sapantaha /sah-pahn-TAH-hah/ n. supposition

sapat /sah-PAHT/ adj. enough

sarhan /sahr-HAHN/ v. shut, close

sarili /sah-REE-lee/ n. self

sariwa /sah-REE-wah/ adj. fresh

sarsa /SAHR-sah/ n. sauce

sasakyan /sah-sahk-YAHN/ n. vehicle

sastre /sahs-TRAY/ n. tailor

sayad /sigh-YAHD/ v. run aground, anchor

sayang /SIGH-yahng/ n. waste

sayawan /sigh-YAHW-ahn/ n. dance

selyo /SAIL-yoh/ n. postage
  stamp
sentimo /SEHN-tee-moh/ n.
  cent, penny
Setyembre /Seht-YEHM-bray/
  n. September
si /see/ part. indicating a
  person; prep. regards, as
  for, in reference to
sibuyas /see-BOO-yahs/ n.
  onion
sikat /SEE-kaht/ n. ray
siklab /sihk-LAHB/ n. flame
siko /SEE-koh/ n. elbow
siksikan /sihk-SEEK-ahn/ n.
  crowd
siga /see-GAH/ n. bonfire
sigalot /see-gah-LOHT/ n.
  quarrel
sigasig /see-GAHS-ihg/ n.
  persistence
sigurado /see-goor-AH-doh/
  adj. sure, certain
siha /SEE-hah/ n. angle
sihang /SEE-hahng/ n. jaw

silangan /see-LAHNG-ahn/
n. east
silaw /SEE-lahw/ n. dazzle,
glare
silid /seel-IHD/ n. room
silipin /see-LEEP-ihn/ v.
peep
silong /SEE-lohng/ n. base-
ment, cellar
silya /SEEL-yah/ n. chair
simbahan /sihm-BAH-hahn/
n. church
sinabik /see-nah-BIHK/ v.
excite, whet
sinag /SEE-nahg/ n. sun-
shine
sinelas /see-NAY-lahs/ n.
slippers
singaw /sihng-AHW/ n.
vapor, steam
singkad /sihng-KAHD/ adj.
exact
singkawan /sihng-kahw-AHN/
v. harness
singsing /sihng-SIHNG/ n.
ring

sining /SEEN-ihng/ n. art
sino /SEE-noh/ int. who?
sinturon /sihn-toor-OHN/
 n. belt
sinulid /see-NOO-lihd/ n.
 thread
sinuman /SEE-noo-mahn/ prn.
 whoever
sipa /SEE-pah/ n. kick
sipain /see-PAH-ihn/ v. kick
sipi /SEEP-ee/ n. copy
sipilyo /see-PEEL-yoh/ n.
 toothbrush
sipon /see-POHN/ n. cold,
 viral infection
sipsipin /sihp-SIHP-ihn/ v.
 sip, suck
sira /SEER-ah/ n. defect
sira /seer-AH/ adj. defec-
 tive, damaged
sirain /seer-AH-ihn/ v.
 damage, break
sitaw /SEE-tahw/ green-bean
siwang /SEE-wahng/ n. slit
siya /she-AH/ prn. he, she

siyam /she-AHM/ num. nine
siyamnapu /shahm-nah-POH/
 num. ninety
siyempre /she-EHM-pray/
 adv. naturally, of course
sobra /SOH-brah/ adv.
 heavily, greatly
sobre /SOH-bray/ n. envelope
subali't /soo-BAHL-iht/
 conj. but
subok /SOO-bohk/ n. test
subukan /soo-BOO-kahn/ v.
 test, try
suka /SOO-kah/ n. vinegar
suka /SOOK-uh/ n. vomit
sukat /SOO-kaht/ n. fit,
 measure (clothes)
sukatan /soo-KAHT-ahn/ v.
 measure, fit, size
suki /SOO-kih/ n. customer,
 client, patron
suklam /sook-LAHM/ n. hate
suklay /sook-LIE/ n. comb
suklayin /sook-lie-IHN/ v.
 comb

sugal /soo-GAHL/ n. gamble
sugalan /soo-gahl-AHN/ v.
 gamble
sugat /SOO-gaht/ n. wound
sugatan /soo-GAHT-ahn/ v.
 wound, injure
suhol /SOO-hohl/ n. bribe
suhulan /soo-HOOL-ahn/ v.
 bribe
sulat /SOO-laht/ n. letter
sulatin /soo-LAHT-ihn/ v.
 write
suliranin /soo-lee-RAHN-
 ihn/ n. problem
sulit /SOOL-iht/ n. experiment, examination
sulok /SOO-lohk/ n. corner
sulsi /sool-SEE/ n. mend
sulsihan /sool-see-HAHN/
 v. mend
sulsulan /sool-SOOL-ahn/
 v. prod, urge, incite
sumabad /soo-mah-BAHD/ v.
 interrupt, intervene
sumabog /soo-MAH-bohg/ v.
 explode, burst

sumakay /soo-mah-KIGH/ v.
 ride
sumama /soo-MAHM-ah/ v. go
 along, go with, accompany
sumandal /soo-mahn-DAHL/ v.
 lean against, recline
sumayaw /soo-mah-YAHW/ v.
 dance
sumbong /soom-BOONG/ n.
 complaint
sumiklab /soo-mihk-LAHB/
 v. flare up, flame
sumingaw /soo-mihng-AHW/
 v. steam, exude vapor
sumpa /soom-PAH/ n. vow
sumuko /soo-MOO-koh/ v.
 surrender
sumumpa /soo-moom-PAH/ v.
 vow, pledge
sundalo /soon-DAHL-oh/
 n. soldier
sundan /soon-DAHN/ v.
 follow, fetch
sundot /soon-DOHT/ n.
 puncture

sundutin /soon-doot-IHN/ v.
 poke, puncture
sungay /SOONG-igh/ n. horns
suntukin /soon-took-IHN/ v.
 box, punch
sunugin /soo-NOOG-ihn/ v.
 burn, char
sunurin /soo-NOOR-ihn/ v.
 follow, obey
suot /soo-OHT/ n. attire
supot /SOO-poht/ n. bag
surbetes /soor-BAY-tehs/
 n. ice cream
suriin /soor-EE-ihn/ v.
 examine
susi /SOO-see/ n. key
susian /soo-SEE-ahn/ v. lock
susunod /soo-soo-NOHD/
 adj. next
sutla /suht-LAH/ n. silk
sutsutan /suht-suht-AHN/
 v. whistle
suutan /soo-OO-tahn/ v.
 put on, wear
suwayin /soo-wigh-IHN/ v.
 disobey

suwerte /SWEHR-tay/ n. luck
suya /soo-YAH/ n. disgust
taas /tah-AHS/ n. height
taba /tah-BAH/ adj. fat
tabi /tah-BEE/ n. side
tabing /TAHB-ihng/ n. curtain, screen
takal /TAH-kahl/ n. measure
takas /TAH-kahs/ n. escape
takasan /tah-KAHS-ahn/ v.
 escape
takbo /tahk-BOH/ v. run
takbuhan /tahk-BOO-hahn/ n.
 run, running event
takda /tahk-DAH/ n. limit
takip /tah-KEHP/ n. cover,
 lid
takpan /tahk-PAHN/ v. cover
takot /TAH-koht/ n. fear
takutin /tah-KOOT-ihn/ v.
 frighten
taga /tah-GAH/ prep. from
tagapagluto /tahg-ah-pahg-
 LOO-toh/ n. cook
tagapagsilbi /tahg-ah-pahg-
 SIHL-bee/ n. waitress

tagapamagitan /tahg-ah-pah-mah-GEE-tahn/ n. mediator

tagapangasiwa /tahg-ah-pahng-ah-SEE-wah/ n. administrator, manager

tagasulat /tahg-ah-SOO-laht/ n. clerk

taginit /tahg-een-IHT/ n. summer

taglagas /tahg-lah-GAHS/ n. fall, autumn

taglamig /tahg-lah-MEHG/ n. winter

taglay /tahg-LIE/ v. possess

tago /tahg-OH/ adj. hidden

tagpi /tahg-PEE/ n. patch

tagpuin /tahg-poo-IHN/ v. meet, encounter

tagubilin /tahg-oo-BEEL-ihn/ n. order, instructions

tagubilinan /tahg-oo-beel-EE-nahn/ v. recommend

tagumpay /tah-GOOM-pie/ n. victory, triumph

tahanan /tah-HAH-nahn/ n. home

tahiin /tah-hee-IHN/ v. sew
tahimik /tah-HEEM-ihk/ adj.
  quiet, peaceful
taimtim /tah-eem-TEEM/ adj.
  sincere
tainga /TAYNG-ah/ n. ear
tala /TAHL-ah/ v. record
talaga /tahl-ah-GAH/ adv.
  really, indeed, truly
talata /tah-LAH-tah/ n.
  sentence
talataan /TAHL-ah-tah-AHN/
  n. paragraph
talatinigan /tahl-AH-tihn-
  ee-gahn/ n. dictionary
talian /tah-LEE-ahn/ v. tie
talisod /tahl-EE-sohd/ v.
  trip, stub one's toe,
  stumble
talon /tah-LOHN/ n. water-
  fall
talsik /tahl-SIHK/ n. splash
talukbong /tah-luhk-BOHNG/
  n. head veil, covering
taluktok /tah-luhk-TOHK/ n.
  top, summit

talumpati /tah-loom-PAHT-
ih/ n. speech
talunin /tah-LOON-ihn/ v.
defeat, best, beat
tama /TAHM-ah/ adj. correct
tama na /TAHM-ah NAH/ adv.
enough
tamaan /tahm-ah-AHN/ v. hit
the target
tamad /tah-MAHD/ adj. lazy
tambol /tahm-BOHL/ n. drum
tampisaw /tahm-pee-SAHW/
v. wade in water
tampo /tahm-POH/ v. sulk,
pout
tanawin /tah-NAHW-ihn/ v.
view, sight
tanawin /TAHN-ahw-ihn/ n.
sight, view, scenery
tandaan /tahn-dah-AHN/ v.
notice, recall
tanga /tahng-AH/ adj. stupid
tangkay /tahng-KIGH/ n. stem
tanggalin /tahng-gahl-IHN/
v. loosen, unfasten

tanggapan /tahng-GAHP-ahn/
 n. office
tanggapin /tahng-gahp-IHN/
 v. receive, accept
tanggihan /tahng-gee-HAHN/
 v. refuse
tanggulan /tahng-GOOL-ahn/
 n. defense
tanghali /tahng-HAHL-ee/
 n. noon
tanghalian /tahng-hahl-EE-
 ahn/ n. lunch
tanghalin /tahng-hahl-IHN/
 v. show, exhibit
tangi /TAHNG-ih/ adj.
 special
tanglaw /tahng-LAHW/ n. lamp
tanglawan /tahng-lahw-AHN/
 v. light, turn on a lamp
tanikala /TAHN-ee-kahl-
 AH/ n. chain
tanim /tah-NEEM/ n. plant
taningan /tahn-IHNG-ahn/
 v. limit
tanod /TAHN-ohd/ n. guard

tanong /tahn-OHNG/ n.
 question
tanso /tahn-SOH/ n. copper
tanungin /tahn-oong-IHN/ v.
 question, ask, inquire
tanyag /tahn-YAHG/ adj.
 popular
tao /TAH-oh/ n. person
taon /tah-OHN/ n. year
tapat /tah-PAHT/ adj. forthright, honest, truthful
tapon /tah-POHN/ n. cork
tapon /TAHP-ohn/ v. discard,
 throw away
tapos /tah-POHS/ adj. complete, through, finished
tapusin /tah-POOS-ihn/ v.
 finish, end, complete
tasa /TAHS-ah/ n. cup
tatakan /tah-tahk-AIIN/ v.
 stamp, mark
tatangnan /tah-tahng-NAHN/
 n. handle
tatay /TAH-tie/ n. father
tatlo /taht-LOH/ num. three

tatlumpu /taht-loom-POH/
 num. thirty
tauhan /tah-OO-hahn/ n.
 officer, official
tawa /TAHW-ah/ n. laughter
tawad /TAHW-ahd/ n. bargain,
 discount
tawagin /tah-WAHG-ihn/ v.
 call
tawaran /tah-WAHR-ahn/ v.
 bargain
tayo /TIE-yoh/ prn. we
tela /TAY-lah/ n. cloth
tikim /tih-KIHM/ n. taste
tiklop /tihk-LOHP/ n. fold
tiklupin /tihk-loop-IHN/
 v. fold
tikman /tihk-MAHN/ v. taste
tiisin /tee-ees-IHN/ v.
 suffer, endure
tilamsikan /tee-lahm-see-
 KAHN/ v. splatter, spill
timba /tihm-BAH/ n. bucket
timbangin /tihm-bahng-IHN/
 v. weigh

timog /TEE-mohg/ n. south
timpiin /tihm-pee-IHN/ v.
 control
tina /TEE-nah/ n. dye
tinapay /tee-NAH-pie/ n.
 bread
tinda /TIHN-dah/ n. goods,
 merchandise
tindahan /tihn-DAH-hahn/ n.
 store, shop
tindig /tihn-DIHG/ n.
 posture, stance
tingga /tihng-GAH/ n. lead
tinggaputi /tihng-GAH-poo-
 TEE/ n. tin
tingin /tihng-IHN/ n. look,
 expression
tingnan /TIHNG-nahn/ v.
 look at
tinik /tccn-IHK/ n. thorn
tinidor /tihn-ih-DOHR/ n.
 fork
tinig /TIHN-ihg/ n. voice
tinitirahan /tee-NEE-teer-
 ah-HAHN/ n. address

tipunin /tee-POON-ihn/ v.
 collect, gather
tirahan /teer-AH-hahn/ n.
 lodging, residence
tiwala /tee-WAHL-ah/ n.
 trust, confidence
tiwasayin /tee-wah-SIGH-
 ihn/ v. calm
tiyak /tee-YAHK/ adj. certain, definite, specific
tiyaga /tee-yuh-GAH/ n.
 perseverance
tiyan /tee-YAHN/ n. stomach
totoo /toh-toh-OH/ adj.
 true
tsaa /chah-AH/ n. tea
tsonggo /CHOHNG-goh/ n.
 monkey
tubig /TOO-bihg/ n. water
tubo /TOO-boh/ n. profit,
 gain, growth
tubusin /too-boos-IHN/ v.
 redeem
tuklasin /tuhk-lahs-IHN/
 v. discover

tuksuhin /tuhk-soo-HIHN/ v.
 tempt, tease
tuktok /tuhk-TOHK/ n. rap,
 knock
tukuyin /too-KUHY-ihn/ v.
 refer to, specify
tugma /TUHG-mah/ n. rhyme
tugon /too-GOHN/ n. reply
tugtog /tuhg-TOOG/ n. music
tugunin /too-goon-IHN/ v.
 reply
tuhod /TOO-hohd/ n. knee
tulay /too-LIE/ n. bridge
tuldok /tuhl-DOHK/ n. dot
tulo /TOO-loh/ n. drip
tulog /TOO-lohg/ n. sleep
tulong /TOO-lohng/ n. help
tulungan /too-LUHNG-ahn/
 v. help
tumakbo /too-mahk-BOH/ v.
 run
tumagos /too-mah-GOHS/ v.
 penetrate
tumahol /too-mah-HOHL/ v.
 bark (dog)

tumalon /too-mah-LOHN/ v.
 jump, dive off
tumanggi /too-mahng-GEE/
 v. refuse, decline
tumapon /too-MAH-pohn/ v.
 spill
tumawid /too-mah-WIHD/ v.
 cross (street, river)
tumbasan /toom-bahs-AHN/
 v. equal
tumpok /toom-POHK/ n. pile
tumubo /too-MOO-boh/ v.
 grow, make a profit
tumuktok /too-muhk-TOHK/
 v. knock
tumulo /too-MOO-loh/ v.
 drip, leak
tumuloy /too-moo-LOHY/ v.
 continue, proceed
tumutol /too-MOO-tohl/ v.
 object, protest
tunawin /too-NOW-ihn/ v.
 melt, dissolve
tunay /TOO-nigh/ adj. au-
 thentic, genuine

tungkod /toong-KOHD/ n.
 cane, walker
tungkol /toong-KOHL/ prep.
 concerning
tungkulin /toong-KOOL-ihn/
 n. duty, obligation
tuntunin /toon-TOON-ihn/
 n. rule
tuos /too-OHS/ n. settlement
tupa /TOO-pah/ n. sheep
tustos /toos-TOHS/ n.
 financial support
tustusan /toos-toos-AHN/
 v. support, finance
tutol /TOO-tohl/ n. objection, protest
tuusin /too-OOS-ihn/ v.
 settle
tuwalya /too-WAHL-yah/ n.
 towel
tuwing /too-WEENG/ adj.
 every
tuyo /too-YOO/ adj. dry
tuyuin /too-yoo-IHN/ v.
 dry

ubas /OO-bahs/ n. grapes
ubo /oo-BOH/ n. cough
ubod /oo-BOHD/ adv.
  considerably
ubuhin /oo-boo-HIHN/ v.
  cough
udyok /ood-YOHK/ n.
  encouragement
udyukan /ood-yuhk-AHN/ v.
  encourage
ugain /oo-gah-IHN/ v. shake
ugali /oo-GAHL-ee/ n. habit
ugat /oo-GAHT/ n. root,
  vein
uhaw /OO-how/ n. thirst
uhawin /oo-HOW-ihn/ v.
  become thirsty, thirst
uhog /OO-hohg/ n. mucus
ulam /OO-lahm/ n. entree,
  main course, food
ulan /oo-LAHN/ n. rain
ulap /OO-lahp/ n. cloud
ulat /OO-laht/ n. report
uli /oo-LEE/ adv. again
ulila /oo-LEE-lah/ n. orphan

uling /OO-lihng/ n. coal
uliran /oo-leer-AHN/ adj.
  ideal
ulitin /oo-LEET-ihn/ v.
  repeat
ulo /OO-loh/ n. head
umaga /oo-MAH-gah/ n.
  morning
umagos /oo-MAH-gohs/ v.
  flow, stream
umaligid /oo-mah-LEE-gihd/
  v. bypass, go around
umalis /oo-mah-LEES/ v.
  depart, leave
umandar /oo-mahn-DAHR/ v.
  function, operate
umanib /oo-MAHN-ihb/ v.
  join
umaraw /oom-AHR-ahw/ v.
  sun, shine
umasa /oom-AHS-ah/ v. place
  hopes on, depend on
umayaw /oom-ahy-AHW/ v.
  won't, will not
umanin /oo-MAHN-ihn/ v.
  imagine

umikot /oo-MEE-koht/ v.
 circle, go around
umidlip /oo-mihd-LIHP/ v.
 nap, snooze
umilag /oo-MEE-lahg/ v.
 avoid, dodge
uminom /oom-ihn-OHM/ v.
 drink
umiyak /oom-ee-YAHK/ v. cry
umpisa /oom-pih-SAH/ v.
 begin, start
umulan /oom-oo-LAHN/ v.
 rain
unahan /oon-ah-HAHN/ v.
 head, be in the lead
unahin /oo-NAH-hihn/ v. do
 first, give priority to
unawain /oon-ah-WAH-ihn/ v.
 understand
ungal /OONG-ahl/ n. roar
unti-unti /oon-TEE oon-TEE/
 adv. gradually
uod /OO-ohd/ n. worm
upa /OO-puh/ n. rental fee
upahan /oo-PAH-hahn/ v.
 rent, hire

upang /OO-pahng/ conj. in
  order to, so that, so as
upo /oo-POH/ v. sit
upos /oo-POHS/ n. cigarette
  stub, ashes
upuan /oo-poo-AHN/ n. seat
uri /UHR-ee/ n. kind, type,
  class, quality
uriin /oo-REE-ihn/ v.
  classify
urong /OO-rohng/ v. recede,
  retreat, draw back
usa /oo-SAH/ n. deer
usapan /oos-ah-PAHN/ n.
  conversation
usapan /oo-SAHP-ahn/ n.
  agreement, compact
usapin /oo-sahp-IHN/ n.
  case, matter, issue
usisain /oo-see-SAH-ihn/
  v. inquire
usok /OO-sohk/ n. smoke
utak /OO-tahk/ n. brain
utang /OO-tahng/ n. debt
utos /OO-tohs/ n. order,
  command

utusan /oo-TOOS-ahn/ v.
  order, command
uwak /oo-WAHK/ n. crow
uwi /oo-WEE/ v. go home
wakas /wah-KAHS/ n. end,
  completion
wakasan /wah-kahs-AHN/ v.
  end, conclude
wagas /wuh-GAHS/ adj. sincere, faithful
waglit /wahg-LIHT/ v. mis-
  place, mislay
wala /wahl-AH/ prn., adv.
  nothing, none
walain /wahl-ah-IHN/ v.
  lose
walang anuman /wahl-AHNG
  ah-noo-MAHN/ ex. you are
  welcome
walang kibo /wahl-AHNG kee-
  BOH/ adj. silent, un-
  responsive, passive
walang kuwenta /wahl-AHNG
  koo-WEHN-tah/ adj. worthless, insignificant

walang-hanggang /wahl-AHNG
 hahng-GAHNG/ adj. forever,
 eternal, endless
walang laman /wahl-AHNG
 luh-MAHN/ adj. empty
walisan /wahl-ees-AHN/ v.
 sweep
walo /wahl-OH/ num. eight
walumpu /wahl-oom-POH/ num.
 eighty
wasakin /wah-sahk-IHN/ v.
 destroy
wasto /wahs-TOH/ adj. correct, up to standard
wastuin /wahs-too-IHN/ v.
 correct, edit
watawat /wah-TAHW-aht/ n.
 flag
welga /WEHL-gah/ n. boycott,
 strike
wika /WEE-kah/ n. language
wili /WEE-lee/ adj. fond
wisikan /wee-seek-AHN/ v.
 spray
yaman /YAH-mahn/ n. wealth

yamutmot /yah-moot-MOHT/ n.
 trash, refuse, rubbish
yari /YAHR-ee/ n. product
yariin /yahr-EE-ihn/ v.
 make, manufacture, build
yata /YAH-tah/ adv. perhaps
yelo /YEH-loh/ n. ice
yumuko /yoo-moo-KOH/ v.
 bow
yungib /yoong-IHB/ n. cave

Part II

ENGLISH/PILIPINO

a /ey/ art. isang
ability /a-BIL-e-ti/ n.
  kakayahan
able /E-bol/ adj. kaya
aboard /a-BORD/ adv. nakasakay, nakaakyat na
about /a-BAWT/ prep. tungkol sa, hinggil sa
absence /AYB-sins/ n.
  kapalyahan, pagpalya
absent /AYB-sint/ adj. pumalya, hindi pumasok
absolutely /ayb-su-LUT-li/
  adv. sakdal, kasukdulan
accept /ayk-SEPT/ v.
  tanggapin
accident /AYK-si-daynt/ n.
  sakuna
accord /a-KORD/ n. kasun-
  duan, intindi, usapan;
  v. payag
according /a-KORD-yng/
  prep. alinsunod sa
accordingly /a-KORD-yng-
  li/ adv. alinsunod

account /a-KAWNT/ n. tuos,
  tuusin; v. sulitin, mag-
  ulat
accuse /a-KYUS/ v. ibintang
accustom /a-KOS-tom/ v.
  magsanay, bihasahin
ache /eyk/ n. kirot; v.
  makirot
across /a-KROS/ adv. sa
  ibayo; prep. sa kibila ng
act /aykt/ v. gumawa; n.
  gawin
action /AYK-syon/ n. galaw,
  kilos
active /AYK-tiv/ adj. ma-
  sipag, maliksi
activity /ayk-TIV-i-ti/ n.
  gawain
actor /AYK-tor/ n. artista
actual /AYK-syul/ adj.
  tunay
actually /AYK-syul-li/ adv.
  talagang-talaga
add /ayd/ v. dagdagan,
  sumahin

address /ayd-DRAYS/ n. tinitirahan; v. talumpatian
admiration /ayd-mir-ES-yon/
n. paghanga
admire /ayd-MYIR/ v.
hangaan
admission /ayd-MIS-yon/ n.
pagpasok, pasukan, pag-
tanggap
admit /ayd-MIT/ v. papasu-
kin, aminin
adopt /a-DAPT/ v. ampunin,
ugaliin
advance /ayd-VAYNS/ v. pa-
unahan, sulong, sumikat;
adj. pauna, antimano
advantage /ayd-VAYN-tij/ n.
pakinabang, kapararakan
adventure /ayd-VENT-syur/
n. pakikipagsapalaran
advertise /AYD-ver-tayz/
v. ipabalita
advice /ayd-VYIS/ n. payo
advise /ayd-VYIZ/ v. payu-
an, bigay-alam, paalam

affair /a-FAYR/ n. pangyayari
affidavit /ayf-i-DEY-vit/
n. apidabit
afford /a-FORD/ v. makaya,
kayang bilhin
afraid /a-FREYD/ adj. takot
after /AYF-tor/ prep. pa-
tapos ng; adv. pagkatapos
after all /AYF-tor AUL/
prep. pagkatapos ng lahat
afternoon /ayf-tor-NUN/ n.
hapon
afterwards /AYF-tor-words/
adv. pagkatapos
again /a-GEN/ adv. uli,
muli
against /a-GENST/ prep. laban sa; adj. tutol, labag
age /eyj/ n. gulang
agent /EYJ-int/ n. ahente,
kinagawa
ago /a-GO/ adv. kanina, sa
nakaraan, noong araw
agony /AYG-o-ni/ n. hapis

agree /a-GRI/ v. payagan
agreement /a-GRI-mant/ n.
 kasunduan, usapan
agriculture /AYG-ri-kolt-
 syur/ n. pagsasaka, pag-
 papatanim
ahead /a-HED/ adv. nauna,
 patungo
aid /eyd/ n. saklolo; v.
 tulungin
aim /eym/ n. layon, tudla,
 tukoy; v. tukuyin, itudla
air /eyr/ n. hangin,
 himpapawid
airplane /EYR-pleyn/ n.
 aeroplano
airport /EYR-port/ n.
 paliparan
airtight /eyr-TAYT/ adj.
 kulob na kulob
alcohol /AYL-ko-hawl/ n.
 alkuhol
alien /EY-li-en/ n. dayo;
 adj. dayuhan
alight /a-LAYT/ v. dumapo

alike /a-LAYK/ adj. kahawig,
 kaparis; adv. magkapareho
alive /a-LAYV/ adj. buhay,
 nabubuhay
all /aul/ adj., prn. lahat,
 lahat ng
all of us /AUL ov os/ ex.
 tayong lahat
all at once /aul ayt WONS/
 adv. nabigla, biglaan
all over /aul OV-or/ adv.
 adv. lahat ng lugar, ka-
 lahatan
allow /a-LAW/ v. hayaan,
 pabayaan, payagan
allowance /a-LAW-ans/ n.
 tustos, baon
almost /AUL-most/ adv.
 halos, munti
aloft /a-LAUFT/ adv. nasa
 itaas, nakaakyat na
alone /a-LON/ adj. nagiisa
along /a-LAWNG/ adv. sabay,
 patungo
alongside /a-lawng-SAYD/
 adv. nakatabi

aloud /a-LAWD/ adv. lakasan
already /aul-RED-i/ adv. na
also /AUL-so/ adv. rin, din,
  pati
although /aul-THO/ conj.
  bagaman
altogether /aul-tu-GE-thor/
  sama-sama, lahat-lahat na
always /AUL-wez/ adv. palagi, lagi
am /em/ v. ay
ambition /aym-BIS-yon/ n.
  pangarap, hangad
ambitious /aym-BIS-yos/
  adj. mapangarap
American /a-MER-i-kan/ n.,
  adj. kano
among /a-MONG/ prep. sa pagitan ng, sa palaot ng
amongst /a-MONGST/ prep. sa
  palaot ng, palaot-laot
amount /a-MAWNT/ n. daghan,
  halaga; v. abutin
amuse /a-MYUZ/ v. libangin
amusement /a-MYUZ-mant/ n.
  libangan

an /ayn/ art. isang
ancient /EYN-chaynt/ adj.
 sinauna, matandang-tanda
ancestor /AYN-says-tor/ n.
 ninuno
and /aynd/ conj. at
anew /a-NIUW/ adv. pani-
 bago, na bago
anger /AYN-gor/ n. galit;
 v. galitin
angle /AYN-gol/ n. siha
angry /AYN-gri/ adj. galit,
 nagagalit, galit na galit
animal /AYN-e-mal/ n. hayop
annoy /a-NOY/ v. buwisitin,
 abalahin, yamutin
another /a-NOTH-or/ prn.,
 adj. iba, isa pa
answer /AYNS-or/ n. sagot;
 v. sagutin
anticipate /ayn-TES-i-peyt/
 v. abangan
antifreeze /AYN-te-friz/ n.
 panlaban sa lamig, pampai-
 nit ng motor ng kotse

anxiety /ayng-ZAY-a-ti/ n.
 balino, balisa
anxious /AYNK-syos/ adj.
 sabik, mabalisa
anybody /EYN-i-bad-i/ prn.
 kahit sino, sinuman
anyhow /EYN-i-haw/ adv.
 kahit paano
anything /EYN-i-theng/
 prn. kahit ano
anyway /EYN-i-wey/ adv. kahit paano, maski na
anywhere /EYN-i-hwer/ adv.
 kahit saan, saan man
apart /a-PART/ adv. bukod
 sa, hiwalay
apartment /a-PART-mant/ n.
 bahay-paupahan
apologize /a-PAUL-a-gayz/
 v. pagpaumanhin
apology /a-PAUL-a-gi/ n.
 paumanhin
appear /a-PIR/ v. lumitaw,
 kamukha
appearance /a-PIR-ens/ n.
 bikas, pakitang-tao

applause /a-PLAUZ/ n.
 palakpak
apple /AYP-ol/ n. mansanas
application /ayp-le-KES-
 yon/ n. aplikasyon, pag-
 tuon
apply /a-PLAY/ v. itapal,
 ituon, umaply, magpresenta
appoint /a-POYNT/ v.
 hirangin
appointment /a-POYNT-mant/
 n. paghirang, tipanan,
 tiyapan
approve /a-PRUV/ v. magpa-
 tibay, payagan
April /EP-ril/ n. Abril
arch /arch/ n. arko, bantok
archway /ARCH-wey/ n. arko,
 pasilyo
are /ar/ v. ay
argue /AR-gu/ v. awayin,
 makipagtalo
argument /AR-gu-mant/ n.
 away, pagtatalo
arise /a-RAYZ/ v. umalsa,
 bumangon

arm /arm/ n. bisig
armor /ARM-or/ n. kalasag
army /AR-mi/ n. hukbo
around /a-RAWND/ prep. pa-
  ligid; adv. sa tabi-tabi
arrange /a-RENJ/ v. ayusin
arrangement /a-RENJ-mant/
  n. ayos, kuntrata
arrest /a-REST/ n. hulihan,
  dakipan; v. hulihin,
  dakipin
arrival /a-RAYV-al/ n.
  pagdating
arrive /a-RAYV/ v. dumating
arrow /ER-o/ n. palaso
art /art/ n. sining
article /AR-te-kol/ n.
  gamit, abubot, pahayag
artificial /ar-te-FIS-yal/
  adj. paimbabaw
artist /AR-test/ n. pintor,
  artista
as /ayz/ adv. katulad, kagaya
as well /ayz WEL/ adv. rin,
  din

as for /AYZ for/ ex. si ___
 naman, ang ___ naman
ash /aysh/ n. abo, upos
ashamed /a-SHEMD/ adj.
 nahiya
aside /a-SAYD/ adv. isan-
 tabi, sa tabi
ask /aysk/ v. magtanong,
 hingi
asleep /a-SLIP/ adv. tulog;
 adj. natutulog
association /a-so-si-AY-
 syon/ n. kapisanan,
 kapatiran
astonish /a-STAN-esh/ v.
 gulatin, biglain
at /ayt/ prep. sa
attack /a-TAYK/ n. salakay,
 lusob; v. salakayin,
 lusubin
attempt /a-TEMPT/ v. subukan, tangkain; n. tangka
attend /a-TEND/ v. dumalo,
 kalingain
attention /a-TEN-syon/ n.
 pansin, kalinga

attract /a-TRAYKT/ v.
 akitin
attraction /a-TRAYK-syon/
 n. bighani, gayuma
audience /AW-di-ens/ n.
 mga manonood
August /AU-gost/ n. Agosto
aunt /aynt/ n. tia
autumn /AW-tom/ n. taglagas
avenue /AYV-e-nu/ n. daan,
 pasyalan
average /AYV-er-ayj/ adj.
 katamtaman, na balasak;
 n. balasak, kainaman
avoid /a-VOYD/ v. umiwas,
 umilag
awake /a-WEK/ adj. gising
awaken /a-WEK-en/ v.
 gisingin
away /a-WEY/ adv. nakaalis,
 nakalayo, lumayo
awful /AU-fol/ adj. kakila-
 kilabot, masama
ax /ayks/ n. palakol
baby /BE-bi/ n. sanggol

back /bayk/ n. likod, li-
kuran; adv. sa likod; v.
kampihan

bad /bayd/ adj. masama

badly /BAYD-li/ adv. di-
maayos, katakot-takot

bag /bayg/ n. supot; v.
isupot

baggage /BAYG-ej/ n. hakot,
dalahan, dala

bake /bek/ v. hurnuhin

balance /BAYL-ans/ n. timbangan, panimbang, kala-
mangan; v. timbangin

ball /baul/ n. bola

band /baynd/ n. kombo, barkada, pangkat, benda, tanda; v. buklurin, magbarkada

bank /baynk/ n. bangko, pampang; v. ibangko

bar /bar/ n. lingkaw, la-
singan

barber /BAR-bor/ n. bar-
bero, mangugupit

bare /ber/ adj. hubo, hubad;
v. hubaran

barely /BER-li/ adv. munti,
 bahagya
bargain /BAR-gen/ n. tawad;
 v. tawaran
barrel /BER-ol/ n. bariles
base /bes/ n. sandigan, ta-
 kad; adj. takaran, imbi;
 v. ibatay
basin /BES-en/ n. palang-
 gana, hilamusan
basis /BES-is/ n. batayan,
 saligan
basket /BAYS-kit/ n. buslo,
 pangnan
bath /bayth/ n. ligo, pa-
 ligo
bathe /bethe/ v. maligo
bathing suit /BETHE-ing
 sut/ n. damit pampaligo
battle /BAYT-ol/ n. laban-
 laban
be; was; been /bi; woz; ben/
 v. maging; ay; ay naging
beam /bim/ n. silaw, sinag,
 tahilan; v. masilaw

bean /bin/ n. sitaw,
 munggo
bear; bore; borne /ber; bor;
 born/ v. tiisin; nagtiis;
 natiis na
beard /bird/ n. balbas
beast /bist/ n. halimaw
beat; beat; beaten /bit;
 bit; BIT-en/ v. bugbugin;
 binugbog; nabugbog; n.
 tibok, palo
beautiful /BYU-te-fol/ adj.
 maganda
beauty /BYU-ti/ n. kagandahan, alindog
because /bi-KAWZ/ conj. sapagka't, mangyari
become; became; become /bi-
 KOM; bi-KEM; bi-KOM/ v.
 maging; naging; nagiging
bed /bed/ n. kama, katre,
 hihigan
before /bi-FOR/ adv. dati;
 prep. bago
beg /beg/ v. palimos

beggar /BEG-er/ n. pulubi
begin; began; begun /bi-
 GEN; bi-GAYN; bi-GON/ v.
 umpisahan; inumpisa; nag-
 umpisa
beginning /bi-GEN-eng/ n.
 pasimula
behavior /bi-HEV-yur/ n.
 asal
behind /bi-HAYND/ prep. sa
 likod ng, sa kabila ng
being /BI-eng/ n. pagkatao
belief /bi-LIF/ n. paniwala
believe /bi-LIV/ v. pani-
 walaan, maniwala
bell /bel/ n. kalembang,
 batingaw
belong /bi-LAUNG/ v. angkin
below /bi-LOW/ prep. sa i-
 baba; adv. ibaba
belt /belt/ n. sinturon
bend; bent; bent /bend;
 bend; bent/ v. baluktutin;
 binaluktot; nabaluktot;
 n. baluktot

beneath /bi-NITH/ prep. sa
  ilalim
beside /bi-SAYD/ prep. sa
  tabi ng; adv. katabi
best /best/ adj. pinakama-
  buti, mas mabuti
better /BET-or/ adj. lalong
  mabuti
between /bi-TWIN/ prep. sa
  pagitan ng; adv. pagitan
beyond /bi-YAND/ prep. lampas, ibayo; adv. lampasan
big /big/ adj. malaki
bike /bayk/ n. bisikleta
bill /bil/ n. kuwenta; v.
  iharap ang kuwenta
bind /baynd/ n. buklod, gapos; v. gapusin
bird /bayrd/ n. ibon
birth /bayrth/ n. pananga-
  nak
bit /bit/ n. kapiraso,
  kapiranting
bite; bit; bitten /bayt;
  bit; BIT-on/ v. kagatin;
  kumagat; nakagat; n. kagat

bitter /BIT-or/ adj. ma-
pait, masaklap
black /blayk/ adj. maitim,
luksa; n. itim
blade /bled/ n. labaha
bleed; bled; bled /blid;
bled; bled/ v. duguin;
dumugo; nagdugo; n. bali-
nguyngoy
bless /bles/ v. bindisyunan
blind /blaynd/ adj. bulag
block /blak/ n. kanto, bara;
v. bumara
blood /blod/ n. dugo
blouse /blaws/ n. blusa
blow; blew; blown /blo; blu;
blon/ v. hipan; humihip;
hinipan; n. hihip, suntok,
dapyo
blow up /blo OP/ v. suma-
bog, pasabugin
blue /blu/ adj. bughaw
board /bord/ n. kapirasong
kahoy, kasanggunian

boast /bost/ v. ipagyabang,
 nagyayabang; n. pagyabang
boat /bot/ n. bangka
body /BAD-i/ n. katawan
boil /boyl/ v. kumulo, pakuluin; n. pagkulo, pigsa
bold /bold/ adj. matapang
boldly /BOLD-li/ adv. ma-
 lakas ang loob
bone /bon/ n. buto
book /bok/ n. aklat
border /BOR-der/ n. hang-
 ganan
born /born/ adj. nanganak
borrow /BAR-o/ v. hiramin,
 sandaliin
both /both/ prn., adj.
 kapuwa
bottle /BAT-ol/ n. bote
bottom /BAT-om/ n. ilalim;
 adj. ilalim na
bound /bawnd/ n. lukso,
 buklod, hangahan; adj.
 ginapos; v. lumukso
boundary /BAWN-dri/ n.
 hangganan

bow /baw/ n. pagyukod, pana,
  laso; v. yumuko
bowl /bol/ n. mangkok
box /baks/ n. kahon; v. suntukin, ikinahon
boy /boy/ n. batang lalaki
brain /bren/ n. utak
branch /braynch/ n. sanga,
  duklay; v. duklayin
brass /brays/ n. tanso
brave /brev/ adj. matapang;
  v. tapangan, kalamayin
bread /brayd/ n. tinapay
breadth /braydth/ n. lapad
break; broke; broken /brek;
  brok; BROK-en/ v. sirain;
  sinira; nasira na; n. bali
breakfast /BRAYK-fost/ n.
  almusal, agahan; v. mag-
  almusal
breath /breth/ n. hininga
breathe /bridth/ v. huminga
brick /brik/ n. tisa
bridge /brij/ n. tulay; v.
  tulayan

bright /brayt/ adj. makislap, maliwanag
bring; brought; brought
/bring; brawt; brawt/ v.
magdala; dinala; nagdala
broad /brawd/ adj. aliwalas,
maluwag, malapad
broadcast /BRAWD-kayst/ v.
magbalita
brother /BRO-thir/ n.
lalaking kapatid
brown /brawn/ adj.
kayumanggi
brush /brosh/ n. eskoba, sipilyo; v. eskubahin, si-
pilyuhin
bucket /BOK-it/ n. timba
build; built; built /bild;
bilt; bilt/ v. yariin;
nayari; yari na
building /BILD-eng/ n.
gusali
bunch /bonch/ n. buwig,
kumpol; v. kumpulin
bundle /BON-dol/ n. bigkis,
tangkas

burn; burned; burned /burn;
 burnd; burnd/ v. sunugin;
 nasunog; sunog na; n. paso
burst; burst; burst /burst;
 burst; burst/ v. magputok;
 pumutok; nagputok
bury /BER-i/ v. ilibing
bus /bas/ n. bus
bush /bosh/ n. tanim, damo,
 talahib
business /BIS-nes/ n. ka-
 lakal, pangangalakal
busy /BIS-i/ adj. maraming
 gawain
but /baht/ conj. nguni't,
 datapwa't, subali't
but once /baht WONS/ ex.
 isang beses lang, minsan
 lang
butcher /BU-cher/ n. ma-
 ngangatay
butter /BOT-or/ n.
 mantekilya
button /BOT-an/ n. butones

buy; bought; bought /bay;
 bowt; bowt/ v. ibili; bu-
 mili; nabili na
by /bay/ prep. sa, ni, sa
 pamamagitan ng
by myself /bay may-SELF/
 adv. magsarili ko
cab /kayb/ n. taksi
cabbage /KAYB-ej/ n.
 repolyo
cage /KEJ/ n. hawla
cake /KEK/ n. puto,
 bibingka, kalamay
calculate /KAYL-ku-let/ v.
 kuwentahin
call /kaul/ v. tawagan;
 n. pagtawag
calm /kalm/ adj. tahimik,
 tiwasay; n. hinahon; v.
 lubagin, tiwasayin, hinahunin
camera /KAYM-or-a/ n. kamera
camp /kaymp/ n. kampo; v.
 humimpil
camp out /kaymp AWT/ v. mag-
 damagan sa kampo

can /kayn/ v. naka, maaari;
 n. lata
canal /ka-NAYL/ n. bambang,
 daluyan
cap /kayp/ n. gora
cape /kep/ n. kapote
capital /KAYP-e-tal/ n. pi-
 nakalunsod, pangulong-
 bayan, puhunan; adj. ulo ng
captain /KAYP-ton/ n.
 kapitan
car /kar/ n. kotse
card /kard/ n. tarheta
care /ker/ n. pagkalinga,
 kandili, pagtingin; v.
 damayin, magmalasakit
careful /KER-fol/ adj. maingat
careless /KER-les/ adj. pabaya, padaskol-daskol, ha-
 laghag
carriage /KER-ej/ n. kalesa
carry /KER-i/ v. buhatin,
 magdala, bitbitin
cart /kart/ n. kareton

case /kes/ n. kahon, lalagyan, usapin, ukulan
cash /kaysh/ n. pera, salapi, "datong"; v. pasuklian
ang pera
castle /KAYS-sol/ n.
kastilyo
cat /kayt/ n. pusa
catch; caught; caught /kech;
kawt; kawt/ v. hulihin;
hinuli; nahuli na
cattle /KAYT-ol/ n. mga baka
cause /kawz/ n. sanhi; v.
pangyarihin
caution /KAW-syon/ n. ingat;
v. ingatan
cave /kev/ n. yungib
cent /saynt/ n. sentimo
center /SAYN-tor/ n. gitna;
v. igitna
century /SAYN-syu-ri/ n.
dantaon
ceremony /SAYR-a-mon-i/ n.
galian
certain /SAYR-ten/ adj.
tiyak, sigurado

chain /chen/ n. tanikala
chair /chayr/ n. silya,
 upuan
chance /chayns/ n. pasumala;
 adj. di-sinadya, alisaga;
 v. magbakasakali
change /chenj/ n. panibago,
 barya, sukli; v. baguhin
character /KER-ik-tor/ n.
 katampatan
charge /charj/ n. sugod,
 tablay, pagbintang; v.
 sumugod, magbintang
charm /charm/ n. gayuma,
 alindog, bighani; v.
 akitin
cheap /chip/ adj. mura
cheat /chit/ v. dayain;
 n. mandaraya
check /chayk/ n. pagmanman,
 tseke; v. manmanan, ampatin
cheer /chir/ n. bunyi; v.
 pagbunyiin
chest /chayst/ n. dibdib,
 baol

chicken /CHIK-on/ n. manok
chief /chif/ n. kabisa,
 datu; adj. pinakapunong
chiefly /CHIF-li/ adv. halos
child /chayld/ n. bata
childish /CHAYLD-esh/ adj.
 musmos
chimney /CHEM-ni/ n. asuhan
choice /choys/ n. pili, bahala; adj. pinakapili
choose; chose; chosen /chuz;
 choz; CHOZ-en/ v. piliin;
 pumili; napili
Christmas /KRIS-mas/ n.
 Pasko
church /church/ n. simbahan
cinema /SEN-i-ma/ n. sine
circle /SER-kol/ n. bilog;
 v. umikot, umaligid
circular /SER-ku-ler/ adj.
 mabilog
citizen /SIT-e-zayn/ n.
 mamamayan
city /SIT-i/ n. lunsod
civilization /si-vil-ay-ZE-
 syon/ n. kabihasnan

civilize /SI-vil-ayz/ v.
 bihasahin
claim /klem/ v. angkinin,
 magdomanda, inyuhin; n.
 domanda
class /klays/ n. uri, klase
classify /KLAYS-e-fay/ v.
 uriin
clay /kle/ n. luad, putik
clean /klin/ adj. malinis,
 dalisay; v. linisin
clear /klir/ adj. malinaw,
 maliwanag
clear up /klir OP/ v. li-
 nawin, maliwanagan
clearly /KLIR-li/ adv. na
 maliwanag
clerk /klirk/ n. tagasulat,
 kawani
clever /KLAY-vor/ adj. marunong, matalino, suwitik
cliff /klif/ n. bangin
climb /klaymb/ n. akyat;
 v. akyatin, gapangin
clock /klak/ n. orasan

close /klos/ adj. malapit;
 v. isara, sarhan
cloth /klawth/ n. tela
clothes /kloz/ n. mga damit,
 bihis, suot
cloud /klawd/ n. alapaap,
 ulap
cloudy /KLAWD-i/ adj. ku-
 limlim, maulap
club /klob/ n. klub, bambu;
 v. bambuhin
coal /kol/ n. uling
coarse /kors/ adj. magalas
coast /kost/ n. dalampasigan; v. padparin, tangayin
coat /kot/ n. amerikana;
 v. itubog
coffee /KAWF-i/ n. kape
coffeepot /KAWF-i-pat/ n.
 kapetera
coin /koyn/ n. barya
cold /kold/ n. lamig, sipon;
 adj. maginaw
collar /KAL-er/ n. kuwelyo
collect /ko-LAYKT/ v. sam-
 samin, tipunin, singilin

collection /ko-LAYK-syon/
n. tipon, katipunan
college /KA-lej/ n. kole-
hiyo
color /KO-ler/ n. kulay;
v. kulayin
coloring /KO-ler-eng/ n.
pangkulay
comb /kom/ n. suklay; v.
suklayin
combination /kam-ben-E-
syon/ n. halo-halo
combine /kam-BAYN/ v. pagsamahin
come; came; come /kom; kem;
kom/ v. pumarito; napar-
ito; nandito na
comeback /KOM-bayk/ n.
pagbabalik
comfort /KOM-fort/ n. ka-
ginhawahan; v. aliwin
command /ko-MAYND/ v. utas-
an, atasan; n. pinagu-
tasan
commerce /KA-mers/ n. ka-
lakal, pangangalakal

commercial /ko-MERS-yal/
 adj. pangkalakalan
committee /ko-MET-i/ n.
 lupon
common /KAM-on/ adj. pangkaraniwan, palasak
common sense /KAM-on SAYNS/
 n. muwang, dilidili
companion /kom-PAYN-yen/
 n. kasama
company /KOM-pa-ni/ n.
 kompanya
comparative /kom-PER-a-tayv/
 adj. mahambing
compare /kom-PAYR/ v.
 ihambing
comparison /kom-PAYR-e-son/
 n. paghambing
compete /kom-PIT/ v. mag-
 paligsahan
competition /kam-pa-TIS-
 yon/ n. paligsahan
competitor /kam-PE-ti-tor/
 n. kasangga, manlalaro
complain /kom-PLEN/ v. magsumbong, magreklamo

complaint /kam-PLENT/ n.
sumbong, reklamo
complete /kam-PLIT/ adj.
ganap, tapos; v. buuin,
tapusin
complicate /KAM-pli-ket/
v. guluhin
compose /kam-POZ/ v. bumuo,
himigan
composer /kam-POZ-or/ n.
kompositor
composition /kam-poz-E-
syon/ n. komposisyon,
likhain
concern /kon-SAYRN/ n. malasakit; v. pinagmalasa-
kitan
condition /kon-DIS-yon/ n.
kalagayan; v. sanayin
confess /kan-FES/ v. mang-
umpisal, aminin, tapatin
confidence /KAN-fi-dens/
n. tiwala
confident /KAN-fi-dent/
adj. paniniwala sa sarili

confuse /kan-FYUZ/ v.
 guluhin
confusion /kan-FYUZ-yan/
 n. kaguluhan
connect /kan-EKT/ v. ikabit,
 pagugpungin, ugnayin
connection /kan-EK-syan/ n.
 ugpungan, kabit, kaugnayan
conquer /KANK-or/ v. lu-
 pigin, manakop
conquest /KAN-kwest/ n.
 paglupig
conscience /KAN-syens/ n.
 budhi
conscious /KAN-syos/ adj.
 may malay
consciousness /KAN-syos-
 nes/ n. malay-tao, ulirat
consider /kan-SID-er/ v.
 pinagiisipan, gunamgunamin
considerable /kan-SID-or-a-
 bol/ adj. ubod na
consideration /kan-sid-or-
 E-syan/ n. pagbibibigay, pakundangan, taros

consulate /KAN-su-let/ n.
 konsulado
contain /kan-TEN/ v.
 lakipan
content /kan-TENT/ adj. nasisiyahan; n. nasiyahan
contentment /kan-TENT-mant/
 n. kasiyahan
contents /KAN-tents/ n.
 laman
continue /kan-TIN-yu/ v.
 ituloy, tumuloy
continuous /kan-TIN-yu-as/
 adj. tuloy-tuloy, panay,
 parati
contract /KAN-traykt/ n.
 kasunduan, kuntrata
control /kan-TROL/ v. timpiin; n. katimpian, hunus-
 dili
convenience /kan-VIN-i-ens/
 n. kaginhawahan
convenient /kan-VIN-i-ent/
 adj. maginhawa
conversation /kan-vayr-SE-
 syon/ n. usapan

cook /kook/ n. kusinero,
 tagapagluto; v. lutuin
cool /kul/ adj. malamig
copper /KAP-or/ n. tanso
copy /KAP-i/ v. huwarin,
 sipiin; n. kopya, sipi
cork /kork/ n. tapon
corkscrew /KORK-skyu/ n.
 pambukas ng tapon
corn /korn/ n. binatog,
 mais
corner /KOR-ner/ n. sulok,
 kanto; v. salukubin
correct /kor-EKT/ adj. tama;
 v. wastuin
cost; cost; cost /kaust;
 kaust; kaust/ v. presyuhan;
 napresyuhan; napresyuhan;
 n. presyo, halaga
cottage /KAT-ej/ n. bahay-
 bahayan
cotton /KAT-en/ n. bulak
cough /kauf/ n. ubo;
 v. inubo
could /kood/ v. ay maaaring

council /KAUN-sel/ n.
 sanggunian
count /kaunt/ v. bilangin;
 n. bilang
country /KAN-tri/ n. bayan,
 bansa
courage /KUR-ej/ n.
 katapangan
course /kors/ n. pagdaan;
 v. dumaan
court /kort/ n. hukuman;
 v. dalawin, ligawin
cousin /KOZ-en/ n. pinsan
cover /KOV-er/ n. takip,
 taklob, kulob; v. takpan,
 takluban, talukbungan
cow /kaw/ n. baka
coward /KAW-ord/ n. duwag;
 adj. naduwag
crack /krayk/ n. lamat;
 v. lamatan, basagin
crash /kraysh/ n. kalabog;
 v. kalabugin
creature /KRI-chur/ n.
 likha, lalang

creep; crept; crept /krip;
 krept; krept/ v. gapangin;
 gumapang; gumapang
crime /kraym/ n. krimen
criminal /KRIM-e-nal/ n.
 salarin; adj. pangsalarin
critic /KRI-tik/ n. kritiko
critical /KRIT-e-kal/ adj.
 palapintasin, masuri, malubha, patawirin
crop /krap/ n. ani
cross /kros/ n. kurus; v.
 tumawid; adj. masungit
crowd /krawd/ n. matao, gitgit; v. siksikan, gitgitan
crown /krawn/ n. korona;
 v. koronahin
cruel /krul/ adj. malupit
crush /krosh/ v. pisain,
 pigain; n. pisa
cry /kray/ v. iyakan; n.
 iyak, hagulgol
cry out /kray AWT/ v.
 ibulalas
cultivate /KOL-ta-vet/ v.
 magsaka, linangin

cultivation /kol-ti-VE-
 syan/ n. pagsasaka
cup /kop/ n. tasa, tason
cure /kyur/ n. hilom; v.
 maghilom, gamutin
curiosity /kyur-i-AS-e-ti/
 n. pagtungaga
curious /KYUR-i-as/ adj.
 mausisa
currency /KUR cn-sl/ n.
 kuwarta
current /KUR-ant/ adj. kasalukuyan; n. agos, saloy
curse /kurs/ n. panunumpa;
 v. sumpain
curtain /KUR-ton/ n. tabing,
 kurtina; v. takluban
curve /kurv/ n. kurba, ka-
 kurbahan; v. kurbahin,
 magbali-baliko
cushion /KUSH-an/ n. kutson
custom /KAS-tom/ n. ugali,
 kaugalian, gawi
customary /KOS-to-mer-i/
 adj. kagawian

cut; cut; cut /kat; kat;
 kat/ v. gupitan; ginupit;
 nagupitan; n. putol, hiwa
cutting /KAT-eng/ adj.
 mapang-uyam
daily /DE-li/ adj. pangaraw-
 araw; adv. araw-araw
damage /DAYM-ej/ n. sira,
 pinsala; v. sirain
damp /daymp/ adj. basa
dampen /DAYM-pen/ v. mabasa
dance /dayns/ v. sumayaw;
 n. sayawan
dancer /DAYNS-or/ n.
 mananayaw
danger /DEN-jor/ n. panganib
dangerous /DEN-jor-os/ adj.
 mapanganib
dare /deyr/ v. hamunin;
 n. hamon
dark /dark/ adj. madilim;
 n. dilim
darken /DAR-ken/ v. dilimin
darkness /DARK-nes/ n.
 karimlan

date /det/ n. petsa, tiyapan; v. dalawin, ligawan,
tiyapin
daughter /DAT-er/ n. anak
na babae
day /de/ n. araw
dead /ded/ adj. patay na
deaf /def/ adj. bingi
deal; dealt; dealt /dil;
delt; delt/ v. makipagayos;
nagkaayos; ayus na; n. pa-
kikipagkasundo
dear /dir/ adj. mahal, masinta
death /deth/ n. kamatayan
debt /dayt/ n. utang
decay /di-KE/ v. bulukin;
n. bulok
deceive /di-SIV/ v. lokohin
December /di-SAYM-bor/ n.
Disyembre
decide /di-SAYD/ v. mapag-
isipan, hatulan
decision /di-SIS-yon/ n.
hatol

decisive /di-SAYS-iv/ adj.
 mapanghatol
declaration /dek-ler-E-syan/
 n. pagpapahayag
declare /di-KLER/ v. ipa-
 hayag
decrease /di-KRIS/ v. ba-
 wasan, awasin; n. bawas
deed /did/ n. titulo
deep /dip/ adj. malalim;
 n. lalim, kalalim-laliman
deer /dir/ n. usa
defeat /di-FIT/ n. kata-
 lunan; v. talunin
defend /di-FEND/ v. ipag-
 tanggol
defense /di-FENS/ n. tanggulan
degree /di-GRI/ n. baitang,
 antas
delay /di-LE/ n. antala,
 laon; v. antalahin
delicate /DEL-e-kat/ adj.
 marupok
delicious /da-LES-yas/ adj.
 masarap

delight /di-LAYT/ n. galak;
 v. nagalak, matuwa
delightful /di-LAYT-fol/
 adj. masiste, natutuwa
deliver /di-LEV-or/ v.
 ipadala
delivery /di-LEV-or-i/ n.
 dinala, pagkahatid
demand /di-MAYND/ v. hil-
 ingin; n. hiling
department /di-PART-mant/
 n. kagawaran
depend on /di-PEND aun/ v.
 umasa sa
dependent /di-PEN-dant/ adj.
 palaasa, di-sariling
depth /depth/ n. lalim
dictionary /DIK-syan-er-i/
 n. talatinigan
die /day/ v. matay
difference /DIF-or-ans/ n.
 kaibahan, kahidwaan
different /DIF-rant/ adj.
 iba
difficult /DIF-e-kolt/ adj.
 mahirap

difficulty /DIF-i-kal-ti/
n. kahirapan, kagipitan
dig; dug; dug /deg; dag;
 dag/ v. hukayin; hinukay;
 naghukay; n. hukayan,
 bungkal
dine /dayn/ v. kain, kumain
dinner /DIN-or/ n. hapunan
direct /day-REKT/ adj. matwid, tuwirang; v. ituro,
 akayin
direction /day-REK-syan/ n.
 dako, tungo, punta, pag-
 gabay
directly /day-REKT-li/
 adv. matuwid
director /day-REK-tor/
 n. patnugot
dirt /dirt/ n. dumi, dungis
dirty /DER-ti/ adj. marumi;
 v. dumihan
disadvantage /des-ayd-VAYN-
 tej/ n. kalamangan
disagree /des-a-GRI/ v.
 di-umayon

disappear /dis-a-PIR/ v.
mawala
disappearance /des-a-PIR-
ans/ n. pagkawala
disappoint /des-a-POYNT/
v. biguin
disappointed /des-a-POYN-
ted/ adj. nabigo
disappointment /des-a-POYNT-
ment/ n. kabiguan
disapprove /des-a-PRUV/ v.
di-inaprubahan
discipline /DIS-a-plen/ n.
pasunod, takdang-asal
discomfort /des-KAM-fort/
n. di-mapakali
discontent /des-kon-TENT/
n. di-nasisiyahan
discontented /des-kon-TEN-
ted/ adj. di-nasiyahan
discover /des-KA-vor/ v.
tuklasin
discovery /des-KAV-or-i/
n. tuklas
discuss /des-KAS/ v. magusap

discussion /des-KAS-yon/ n.
 pagusapan, salitaan
disease /des-IZ/ n. sakit
disgust /des-GAST/ n. suya,
 pagkamuhi; v. nasuya
disgusted /des-GAST-ed/ adj.
 suyang-suya
dish /desh/ n. pingan, ulam;
 v. sandukin
dismiss /dis-MES/ v. itini-
 walag, pinaalis
disobey /dis-o-BE/ v.
 suwayin
displease /des-PLIZ/ v.
 galitin
distance /DIS-tans/ n.
 agwat, layo
distant /DIS-tant/ adj.
 malayo
distinguish /des-TIN-gwesh/
 v. uriin, pinasikat
district /DIS-trekt/ n. pook
disturb /dis-TORB/ v. gambalain, abalahin
disturbance /des-TOR-bans/
 n. gambala, kaabalahan

dive /dayv/ v. tumalon;
n. talon
divide /di-VAYD/ v. hatiin,
bahagihin
division /di-VIS-yan/ n.
palahatian, sangay
do; did; done /du; did; don/
v. gawin; gumawa; nagawa
do well /du WEL/ v. gawin
mabuti, sumikat, umasenso
do without /du weth-AWT/ v.
iniraos maski wala
doctor /DAK-tor/ n. mang-
gagamot
dog /daug/ n. aso
dollar /DAL-er/ n. dolyar
door /dor/ n. pinto
doorway /DOR-we/ n. pintuan,
labasan
dot /dat/ n. tuldok; v.
tuldukan
double /DO-bel/ adj. ibayo;
v. doblihin
doubt /dawt/ n. alinlangan;
v. nagalinlangan

doubtful /DAWT-fol/ adj.
 atubili
doubtless /DAWT-les/ adv.
 siguro
down /dawn/ adv. ibaba
downstairs /dawn-STERS/ adv.
 sa silong, ibaba ng bahay
downwards /DAWN-words/ adv.
 sa ibaba, lusong
dozen /DOZ-en/ n. dosena
drag /drayg/ v. hilahin;
 n. hilahod
draw; drew; drawn /drau;
 dru; draun/ v. iguhit;
 iginuhit; iginuhit
drawback /DRAU-bayk/ n. pag-
 urong; v. inurong
drawer /dror/ n. kahon
dream; dreamed; dreamed
 /drim; drimd; drimd/ v. i-
 panaginip; nanaginip; na-
 panaginip; n. panaginip
dress /dres/ n. bestida, bihis, suot, pananamit; v.
 bihisan, damitan

drink; drank; drunk /drenk;
 draynk; dronk/ v. inom;
 uminom; uminom; n. inumin
drive; drove; driven /drayv;
 drov; DREV-an/ v. magmaneho; minaneho; minaneho;
 n. namasyal sa kotse
drop /drap/ v. tumba, i-
 bagsak; n. patak
drown /drawn/ v. lunurin
drum /drom/ n. tambol;
 v. magtambol
dry /dray/ adj. tuyo;
 v. tuyuin, matuyo
duck /dak/ n. bibi, itik;
 v. umilag
due /du/ adj. napapaso
due to /du tu/ conj. dahil
 sa
dull /dal/ adj. mapurol
during /DUR-eng/ prep.
 habang
dust /dast/ n. alikabok;
 v. paspasan, pagpagin
duty /DU-ti/ n. tungkulin

each /itch/ prn., adj.
 bawa't
eager /I-ger/ adj. sabik,
 duhapang
eagerly /I-gor-li/ adv. na-
 sasabik
ear /ir/ n. tainga
early /ER-li/ adj. maaga;
 adv. maagang-maaga
earn /ern/ v. kitain
earnest /ERN-ast/ adj. buo
 sa loob
earth /erth/ n. lupa
earthly /ERTH-li/ adj. maka-
 lupa, panglupa
ease /iz/ n. kaginhawahan;
 v. gaanan
easily /IZ-a-li/ adv. mada-
 lian
east /ist/ n. silangan;
 adv. silanganan
eastern /IS-torn/ adj.
 silangan
easy /IZ-i/ adj. madali,
 magaan

eat; ate; eaten /it; et; IT-
an/ v. kainin; kumain; kumain
edge /edj/ n. gilid, bingit
educate /E-ju-ket/ v. pa-
aralin
education /e-ju-KE-syan/ n.
pinagaralan, pagtuturo
educational /ed-ju-KE-syon-
al/ adj. may aral
effect /a-FEKT/ n. bisa, ka-
labasan; v. pangyarihin
effective /a-FEK-tiv/ adj.
mabisa
efficiency /a-FI-syayn-si/
n. katalaban, kahusayan
efficient /a-FIS-yant/ adj.
matalab, masinop
effort /EF-ort/ n. pag-
pursige
egg /eg/ n. itlog
eight /et/ num. walo
eighteen /et-TIN/ num.
labing-walo
eighty /ET-i/ num. walumpu

either /I-thor/ prn., adj.
 kahit alin sa
elastic /i-LAYS-tek/ adj.
 igkasin
elder /AYL-dor/ n., adj.
 panganay
elect /i-LEKT/ v. ihalal;
 adj. halal na
election /i-LEK-syan/ n.
 halalan
electric /a-LEK-trayk/ adj.
 madagitab, dagisikin
electricity /a-lek-TRIS-e-
 ti/ n. dagitab, kuryente
elephant /EL-a-fant/ n.
 elepante
eleven /i-LE-van/ num.
 labing-isa
else /els/ adv. pa
elsewhere /ELS-hwer/ adv.
 sa ibang lugar
embarrass /im-BER-as/ v.
 mapahiya
emergency /i-MAYR-jen-si/
 n. emerhensya

empire /EM-payr/ n. lupain
employ /em-PLOY/ v. pina-
trabaho, gamitin
employee /em-PLOY-i/ n. mga
katulong, kawani
employer /em-PLOY-or/ n. may-
ari, namumuhunan, amo
employment /em-PLOY-mant/
n. pagkakakitaan
empty /EMP-ti/ adj. walang
laman; v. todasin, ubusin
enclose /en-KLOZ/ v. mag-
lakip
encourage /en-KUR-ej/ v.
udyukan
encouragement /en-KUR-ej-
mant/ n. udyok
end /end/ n. dulo, wakas,
katapusan; v. wakasan,
tapusin
endless /END-las/ adj.
walang-hanggang
enemy /EN-a-mi/ n. kalaban;
adj. magkalaban, magkagalit
engine /EN-jin/ n. makina

engineer /en-jen-IR/ n.
inhinyero

English /AYNG-lesh/ n.,
adj. Inggles

enjoy /in-JOY/ v. magpaka-
saya

enjoyment /in-JOY-mant/ n.
kasiyahan, katuwaan

enough /i-NOF/ adj. sapat;
adv. tama na

enter /EN-tar/ v. ipasok

entertain /en-tor-TEN/ v.
pakiharapan, libangin

entertainment /en-tor-TEN-
mant/ n. aliwan

entire /in-TAY-or/ adj.
buo

entirely /in-TAY-or-li/
adv. mabuo

entrance /EN-trayns/ n.
pasukan

envelope /EN-va-lop/ n.
sobre

envious /EN-vi-os/ adj. mainggitin

envy /EN-vi/ n. ingit, pa-
naghili; v. inggitin, pa-
naghilian
equal /I-kwal/ adj. katum-
bas; v. tumbasan
equality /i-KWAL-a-ti/ n.
katumbasan
equally /I-kwal-i/ adv.
pantay-pantay
escape /es-KEP/ n. takas;
v. takasan
especially /is-PESH-yal-i/
adv. mas pa, lalo na
essence /ES-ans/ n. buod
essential /i-SEN-syal/ adj.
kailangan-kailangan
even /I-van/ adj. pantay;
v. pantayin
evening /IV-neng/ n. gabi
event /i-VENT/ n. pangya-
yari
ever /EV-or/ adv. pag, man,
panay
every /EV-ri/ adj. tuwing
everybody /EV-ri-bad-i/
prn. lahat-lahat

everyday /EV-ri-de/ adj.
  pangaraw-araw
everyone /EV-ri-wan/ prn.
  bawa't isa-isa
everything /EV-ri-theng/
  prn. lahat
everywhere /EV-ri-hwer/ adv.
  lahat ng dako
evil /I-val/ adj. masama
exact /ik-SAYKT/ adj. husto,
  singkad; v. hustuhan
exactly /ik-SAYKT-li/ adv.
  na husto
examination /ik-saym-in-E-
  syan/ n. suri, pagsulit
examine /ik-SAYM-an/ v.
  suriin, butingtingin
example /ik-SAYM-pol/ n.
  halimbawa
excellence /EK-sa-lens/ n.
  galing, giting
excellent /EK-sa-lent/ adj.
  magaling
except /ik-SEPT/ prep. mali-
  ban sa; v. pinagpaliban

exception /ik-SAYP-syan/ n.
 kataliwasan
excess /EK-says/ n. labis
excessive /ik-SES-iv/ adj.
 labis-labis
exchange /iks-CHENJ/ v. pa-
 litan; n. pagpalit
excite /ik-SAYT/ v. sinabik
excitement /ik-SAYT-mant/
 n. pagkalugod
excursion /iks-KUR-syan/ n.
 pagpasyal
excuse /iks-KYUZ/ v. patawarin; n. dahilan, katu-
 wiran
exercise /EK-sor-sayz/ n.
 hersisyo; v. hersisyuhin
exist /ek-ZIST/ v. mamuhay
existence /ek-ZIS-tans/ n.
 kabuhayan
expect /iks-PEKT/ v. inaabangan, hinagapin
expectation /ek-spek-TE-
 syan/ n. pagabang, hinagap
expense /ik-3PENS/ n. gastos, gugulin

expensive /iks-PEN-siv/
adj. mahal
experience /eks-PIR-i-ens/
n. karanasan; v. dumanas,
lasapin
experiment /ik-SPER-a-ment/
n. esperimento; v. suriin,
sulitin
explain /iks-PLEN/ v. ipaliwanag
explanation /eks-pla-NE-
syan/ n. pagpaliwanag
explode /eks-PLOD/ v.
sumabog
explorer /iks-PLOR-er/ n.
tagasaliksik
explosive /eks-PLO-siv/ n.
paputok; adj. pampaputok
express /iks-PRES/ n., adj.
pagpapahatid; v. hayag,
salitain
extend /ik-STEND/ v. dug-
tungan, palugitan
extension /iks-TEN-syan/ n.
karugtong, palugit

extensive /iks-TEN-siv/
 adj. malawak
extent /iks-TENT/ n. lawak
extra /EKS-tra/ adj. labis;
 n. kalabisan, kapalit
extraordinary /eks-TROR-din-
 er-i/ adj. pambihira
extreme /ek-STRIM/ adj. suk-
 dulin; n. sukdulan
extremely /ek-STRIM-li/
 adv. sakdal
eye /ay/ n. mata
face /fes/ n. mukha; v. i-
 harap, sagupain
fact /faykt/ n. katotohanan
factor /FAYK-tor/ n. kabuo
factory /FAYK-tor-i/ n.
 gawaan
fade /fed/ v. kupas, ngupas,
 pumupusyaw
fail /fel/ v. matalo, bi-
 guin, bumagsak
failure /FEL-yur/ n. kabiguan, "bagsak"

faint /fent/ adj. hilo; n.
himatay; v. himatayin
fair /fer/ adj. patas; n.
perya
fairly /FER-li/ adv. medyo
faith /feth/ n. pananam-
palataya
faithful /FETH-fol/ adj.
wagas
fall; fell; fallen /faul;
fel; FAUL-en/ v. mahulog;
nahulog; nahulog; n. pag-
kabagsak, taglagas
false /fauls/ adj. huwad
familiar /fa-MIL-yar/ adj.
magkakilala, datihan
family /FAYM-a-li/ n. maganak, angkan
famous /FEM-as/ adj. ban-
tog, tanyag
fan /fayn/ n. pamaypay,
bentilador, tagahanga
fancy /FAYN-si/ adj. ma-
kalakuti
far /far/ adj., adv. malayo

far from /far from/ adj.,
 adv. layong-layo
farm /farm/ n. taniman,
 sakahan; v. sakahin
farmer /FARM-or/ n. mag-
 sasaka
farther /FAR-thor/ adj.
 dulong-dulo; adv. malayo pa
fashion /FAY-syan/ n. moda,
 kalakaran; v. hugisan
fast /fayst/ adj. mabilis;
 adv. madali; v. di-kumain
fasten /FAYS-an/ v. ikabit
fat /fayt/ adj. mataba;
 n. taba
fate /fet/ n. kapalaran,
 suwerte
father /FA-thor/ n. ama
fault /falt/ n. bisala,
 kasalanan
favor /FE-vor/ n. biyaya;
 v. lawitan
favorable /FE-vor-a-bol/
 adj. mapalad

favorite /FE-vor-it/ adj.,
n. paborito
fear /fir/ n. takot, pan-
gamba, hilakbot; v. pan-
gambahan
feast /fist/ n. kainan;
v. magpakabusog
feather /FETH-or/ n.
balahibo
February /FEB-ru-er-i/ n.
Pebrero
feed; fed; fed /fid; fayd;
fayd/ v. pakainin; pina-
kain; nagpakain; n. pakain
feel; felt; felt /fil; felt;
felt/ v. damahin; dinama;
nadama
feeling /FIL-eng/ n. loobin,
damdamin, kutob, dilidili;
maramdamin
fellow /FEL-ow/ n. mama,
pare; adj. kapwa
female /FI-mel/ n. babae;
adj. pambabae

fence /fens/ n. bakod, ha-
 lang; v. halangan
fever /FI-vor/ n. lagnat
feverish /FI-vor-ish/ adj.
 nilalagnat
few /fiw/ adj. kaunti;
 prn. ilan-ilan
field /fild/ n. bukid
fierce /firs/ adj. mabagsik
fifteen /fef-TIN/ num.
 labinlima
fifty /FEF-ti/ num. limampu
fight; fought; fought /fayt;
 faut; faut/ v. labanan;
 lumaban; naglaban; n. laban, suntukan
figure /FIG-yur/ n. anyo,
 laraw, korti, hitsura;
 v. kuwentahin, anyuin
Filipino /fel-a-PI-no/ n.,
 adj. pinoy
fill /fil/ v. punuin, apawan; n. pagkapuno
fill up /fil AP/ v. punuin,
 apawan, lulanan

film /film/ n. pila, pelikula; v. ritratuhan
find; found; found /faynd;
fawnd; fawnd/ v. mamulot;
nakapulot; nakapulot;
n. nakita
fine /fayn/ adj. mapino, mataas ang uri, "o.k. lang";
n. multa; v. multain
finger /FIN-gor/ n. daliri
finish /FIN-esh/ n. wakas,
katapusan, tubog; v. ta-
pusin
fire /FAY-ir/ n. apoy, sunog
firearm /FAYR-arm/ n. armas
firm /firm/ adj. matatag,
matibay; n. kompanya
firmly /FERM-li/ adv. naka-
pirme
first /ferst/ adj. ikaisa,
pangisa; adv. sa una
fish /fish/ n. isda
fit /fit/ n. sukat; v. i-
sukat; adj. angkop

fitting /FIT-eng/ n. pagsusukat; adj. ugma
five /fayv/ num. lima
fix /fiks/ v. ayusin, kumpunihin
flag /flayg/ n. watawat,
 bandila
flame /flem/ n. ningas;
 v. sumiklab
flash /flaysh/ n. siklab;
 v. sumiklab
flashlight /FLESH-layt/
 n. tanglaw
flat /flat/ adj. pipis;
 n. kapatagan
flavor /FLE-vor/ n. linamnam
flesh /flesh/ n. laman
float /flot/ v. padparin,
 lutang
flood /flad/ n. baha;
 v. bahain
floor /flor/ n. sahig,
 palapag
flour /FLAW-or/ n. harina

flow /flo/ n. anod, daloy;
 v. dumaloy
flower /FLAW-or/ n. bulaklak; v. mamulaklak
fly; flew; flown /flay; flu;
 flon/ v. liparin; lumipad;
 nakalipad; n. langaw,
 bangaw
focus /FO-kas/ n. tuon;
 v. ituon
fold /fold/ n. tiklop, lupi;
 v. tiklupin
follow /FAL-o/ v. sunurin,
 sundin
follower /FAL-o-er/ n. taga-
 sunod, alagad
fond /fand/ adj. wili
food /fud/ n. pagkain, ulam
fool /ful/ n. gago, gaga,
 bobo; v. lokohin, bolahin,
 lamangan
foolishness /FUL-esh-nas/
 n. kalokohan, kagaguhan
foot /foet/ n. paa
football /FOET-bal/ n. si-
 pang bola

for /foer/ prep. para sa,
sa; conj. kaya
forbid; forbade; forbidden
/for-BID; for-BAYD; for-
BID-an/ v. pagbawalan; pi-
nagbawalan; nagbawal
force /fors/ n. dahas, isig;
v. pilitin, tungkabin
foreign /FOR-in/ adj. dayuhan
foreigner /FOR-in-or/ n.
dayo, banyaga
forget; forgot; forgotten
v. limutin; nakalimutan;
nakalimutan na
forgive; forgave; forgiven
/for-GIV; for-GEV; for-GI-
van/ v. patawarin; pina-
tawad; napatawad
fork /fork/ n. tinidor,
sangahan; v. magkasanga
form /form/ n. anyo, hugis,
hubog; v. hugisan, hulma-
hin, hubugin
formal /FOR-mal/ adj. pormal

formally /FOR-mal-i/ adv.
  pormalan
former /FOR-mor/ adj. dati
forth /forth/ adv. tumungo
fortune /FOR-chan/ n. kayamanan, kapalaran
forty /FOR-ti/ num. apat-
  napu
forward /FOR-ward/ adj.,
  adv. mauna; v. unahin, i-
  padala
forwards /FOR-wards/ adv.
  nauuna
four /for/ num. apat
fourteen /for-TIN/ num.
  labing-apat
frame /frem/ n. kuwadro, balangkas, bastagan; v. i-
  kuwadro
free /fri/ adj. malaya; v.
  palayain, bitawan
freedom /FRI-dam/ n. kalayaan
freely /FRI-li/ adv. kusang
  loob

freeze; froze; frozen /friz;
 froz; FRO-zan/ v. iyelo;
 iniyelo; yelado
frequent /FRI-kwent/ adj.
 madalas; v. pinaglalagian
frequently /FRI-kwent-li/
 adv. kadalasan
fresh /fresh/ adj. sariwa
Friday /FRAY-de/ n. Biyernes
friend /frend/ n. kaibigan
friendly /FREND-li/ adj.
 mapagkaibigan
friendship /FREND-ship/ n.
 palagayan, pakikipagka-
 ibigan
fright /frayt/ n. sindak,
 takot
frighten /FRAY-tan/ v.
 takutin
from /fram/ prep. galing sa
front /front/ n. harapan,
 unahan; adj. sa harapan
frost /fraust/ n. yelo
frosty /FRAUS-ti/ adj.
 mayelo

fruit /frut/ n. prutas,
 bungang-kahoy
fry /fray/ v. pirituhin
full /fol/ adj. puno, tigib,
 puspos
fun /foan/ n. kasayahan,
 katuwaan
funeral /FYU-nor-al/ n.
 paglilibing
funny /FO-ni/ adj. katawa-
 tawa, nakakatuwa
fur /fur/ n. lanilya
furnish /FUR-nesh/ v. lagyan
 ng mga kasangkapan
furniture /FUR-na-chur/ n.
 kasangkapan, muwebles
further /FUR-ther/ adj.
 malayu-layo; adv. palayu-
 layo
future /FYU-chor/ n. hinaharap
gain /gen/ n. tubo; v.
 tubuin
gallon /GAY-lan/ n. galon

gamble /GAYM-bol/ n. sugal;
 v. sugalan
game /gem/ n. laruan
gap /gayp/ n. puwang
garage /gar-AJ/ n. garahe
garbage /GAR-bej/ n. basura,
 layak, yamutmot
garden /GAR-dan/ n. hala-
 manan
gas /gays/ n. buhog, kabag
gate /get/ n. tarangkahan
gateway /GET-we/ n. pasukan
gather /GAY-ther/ v. sam-
 samin, tipunin, nagkasama-
 sama
gay /ge/ adj. masaya, ma-
 sigla; n. bakla
general /JEN-or-al/ adj.
 panlahatan; n. lahatan,
 heneral
generally /JEN-or-al-i/
 adv. kalahatan
generous /JEN-or-as/ adj.
 mapagbigay, maawa
gentle /JEN-tal/ adj. ma-
 bini, butihin

gentleman /JEN-tal-mayn/ n.
 maginoo
gently /JENT-li/ adj. atay-
 atay, dahan-dahan
get; got; gotten /get; gat;
 GAT-an/ v. ikuha; kinuha;
 nakuha
get along /gayt a-LAWNG/ v.
 makisama, iraos
get off /gayt AUF/ v. umi-
 bis
get out /gayt AWT/ v. umalis, nakawala
get up /gayt AP/ v. bu-
 mangon
get to know /gayt tu NO/
 v. nakilala
girl /gerl/ n. babae, ba-
 tang babae, dalaga
give; gave; given /giv; gev;
 GIV-an/ v. ibigay; binigay;
 nagbigay
give away /giv a-WE/ v.
 pinamigay
give in /giv IN/ v. binigay
 na rin, pumayag sa huli

give up /giv AP/ v. pinau-
baya
glad /glayd/ adj. natuwa
gladly /GLAYD-li/ adv. maluwag sa loob
glass /glays/ n. salamin,
baso
glorious /GLOR-i-as/ adj.
luwalhati
glory /GLOR-i/ n. kaluwalhatian; v. luwalhatiin
go; went; gone /go; went;
gaon/ v. magpunta; pumunta;
nagpunta
go along /go a-LAONG/ v.
sumama, makisama
go away /go a-WE/ v. umalis
go back /go BAYK/ v. bumalik, inurong
go by /go BAY/ v. sumaglit,
silayan
go on /go AN/ v. sumulong,
tumuloy; ex. sige
go between /go bi-TWIN/ v.
nakipamagitan; n. tagapa-
magitan

God /gad/ n. Bathala
goddess /GAD-es/ n. diwata
gold /gold/ n. ginto
golden /GOL-den/ adj.
 ginintuan
gold-plated /gold PLE-tad/
 adj. tubog sa ginto
good /geud/ adj. mabuti,
 mabait
good-bye /geud BAY/ n. paalam; ex. aalis na ako
goodness /GEUD-nas/ n. ika-
 bubuti, kabutihan
good will /geud WIL/ n.
 pakikipagmabutihan
goods /geudz/ n. mga tinda,
 bilihin
govern /GAV-ern/ v. sakupin,
 pamamahala
government /GAV-orn-mant/
 n. pamahalaan
governor /GAV-ern-or/ n.
 gobernador
grace /gres/ n. biyaya; v.
 biyayaan

graceful /GRES-fol/ adj.
 malantik
gradual /GRAY-dyu-al/ adj.
 dahan-dahan
gradually /GRAY-dyu-al-li/
 adv. unti-unti
grain /gren/ n. trigo, butil
grammar /GRAY-mor/ n.
 balarila
grand /graynd/ adj. malawak,
 lubusang
grass /grays/ n. damo
grateful /GRET-fol/ adj. pag-
 tanaw ng utang na loob
grave /grev/ n. pantiyon;
 adj. malubha, malala
grease /gris/ n. mantika,
 sabo; v. langisan
great /gret/ adj. dakila
greatly /GRET-li/ adv. na
 mahalaga
greatness /GRET-nas/ n.
 kadakilaan
greed /grid/ n. imbot, siba,
 katakawan

greedy /GRI-di/ adj. sakim,
 masunggab
green /grin/ adj. luntian
greet /grit/ v. salubungin,
 batiin, kumustahin
greeting /GRIT-eng/ n. bati,
 kumustahan
grey /gre/ adj. abuhin
grind; ground; ground
 /graynd; grawnd; grawnd/
 v. durugin; dinurog; na-
 durog na; n. giniling
grope /grop/ v. kapain,
 mag-apuhap
ground /grawnd/ n. lupa; v.
 sayad, gilingin
group /grup/ n. pangkat,
 kuponan; v. pagsamahin
grow; grew; grown /gro; gru;
 gron/ v. patubuin; tumubo;
 nagtubo
grown-up /gron AP/ n., adj.
 nasagulang
growth /groth/ n. tubo,
 yabong

guard /gard/ n. tanod, bantay, taliba; v. bantayan, tumanod

guess /ges/ v. hulaan; n. hula

guest /gest/ n. panauhin

guide /gayd/ n. patnubay, gabay; v. patnubayin, akayin

guilt /gilt/ n. kasalanan

guilty /GIL-ti/ adj. makasalanan

gun /goen/ n. baril

habit /HAY-bit/ n. ugali, gawi

hair /her/ n. buhok

half /hayf/ n., adv., adj. kalahati

half an hour /hayf ayn AW-or/ n. kalahating oras

hall /haol/ n. bulwagan, salas

hammer /HAY-mar/ n. martilyo; v. pukpukin

hand /hend/ n. kamay; v. abutan

handful /HEND-fol/ n. dakot
handkerchief /HEN-kar-chif/
 n. panyo
handle /HEN-dal/ n. hawakan,
 tatangnan
handy /HEN-di/ adj. masilbi
hang; hung; hung /hayng;
 hang; hang/ v. sabitan;
 isinabit; nasabit
happen /HAY-pan/ v. mangyari
happily /HAYP-a-li/ adv.
 napaligaya
happy /HAY-pi/ adj. maligaya
harbor /HAR-bor/ n. daungan
hard /hard/ adj. matigas,
 mahirap
hardly /HARD-li/ adv.
 bahagya
harm /harm/ n. saktan
harvest /HAR-vest/ n. ani,
 gapasan; v. anihin, gapasin
haste /hest/ n. dalos, pag-
 tutulin, pagmamadali
hasten /HES-an/ v. dali-
 daliin, nagmamadali

hastily /HES-te-li/ adv.
 padalos-dalos
hat /hayt/ n. gora, samba-
 lilo
hate /het/ n. poot, suklam;
 v. masuklam
hatred /HET-rad/ n. poot,
 suklam
have; had; had /hayv; hayd;
 hayd/ v. mayroon; nagka-
 roon; mayroon na
have been /hayv BEN/ v. ay
 nagiging
have to /HAYV tu/ v. kai-
 langan mag____
hay /he/ n. dayami
he /hi/ prn. siya
head /hed/ n. ulo; v. unahan
headlong /HED-laong/ adv.
 nakahilera
heal /hil/ v. maghilom
health /helth/ n. kalusugan
healthy /HEL-thi/ adj. malusog

heap /hip/ n. bunton, ipon, tumpok; v. ibunton, mag-tumpok

hear; heard; heard /hir; herd; herd/ v. marinig; nadinig; nadinig

heart /hart/ n. puso

heartily /HART-e-li/ adv. masinsinan, buong-puso

heat /hit/ n. init

heaven /HE-van/ n. langit

heavenly /HE-van-li/ adj. makalangit

heavily /HEV-e-li/ adv. sobrang-sobra

heavy /HEV-i/ adj. mabigat

height /hayt/ n. taas

help /help/ n. tulong; v. tulungan, daluhan

helpful /HELP-fol/ adj. matulungin

helpless /HELP-las/ adj. wa-lang magawa, nakalugmok

her /her/ prn. niya; adj. kanyang

here /hir/ adv. dito, dini
hers /herz/ adj. kanyang,
 niya
herself /her-SELF/ prn. kanyang sarili, sarili niya
hesitate /HEZ-i-tet/ v. nag-
 aatubili, bantulot
hi /hay/ ex. huy!
hide; hid; hidden /hayd;
 hid; HID-an/ v. itago;
 tinago; nagtago
high /hay/ adj. mataas, ma-
 tayog; adv. sa taas
highly /HAY-li/ adv. tini-
 tingala
highway /HAY-we/ n. daan
 pangmalayuan
hill /hil/ n. burol, punso,
 tugatog
hillside /HIL-sayd/ n. libis
hinder /HIN-dor/ v. had-
 langan
hire /hayr/ n. upa; v. u-
 pahan
his /hiz/ adj. kanyang, niya

historic /his-TOR-ik/ adj.
 makasaysayan
history /HES-tor-i/ n.
 kasaysayan
hit; hit; hit /hit; hit;
 hit/ v. hampasin; hinampas;
 nahampas; n. tamaan
hold; held; held /hold;
 held; held/ v. hawakan;
 hinawakan; nahawakan; n.
 hawak, kapit, taban
hole /hol/ n. butas
holiday /HAL-e-de/ n. pis-
 tang opisyal, araw ng
 pangilin
hollow /HAL-o/ n. guwang;
 adj. humpak
holy /HO-li/ adj. banal
home /hom/ n. tahanan, pa-
 mamahay; adj. pantahanan;
 adv. nasa bahay
honest /A-nest/ adj. ma-
 tapat
honesty /A-nes-ti/ n.
 katapatan

honor /A-nor/ n. dangal, karangalan; v. iginalang,
  parangalan
honorable /A-nor-a-bol/ adj.
  marangal, kagalang-galang
hook /huk/ n. pangalawit,
  sabitan; v. isabit
hope /hop/ n. pagasa; v.
  umasa
hopeful /HOP-fol/ adj.
  maasa
hopeless /HOP-las/ adj.
  walang pagasa
horizon /ho-RAY-zan/ n.
  kagiliran
horse /hors/ n. kabayo
hospital /HAS-pe-tol/ n.
  ospital, pagamutan
host /host/ n. may parangal;
  v. magparangal
hot /hat/ adj. mainit, maalinsangan
hotel /ho-TEL/ n. otel
hour /awr/ n. oras

house /haws/ n. bahay, tirahan; v. patirahin
household /HAWS-hold/ n.
sambahayan; adj. pantaha-
nan
housewife /HAWS-wayf/ n.
babaeng pantahanan
how /haw/ adv. kung gaano;
ex. paano?
however /haw-E-vor/ conj.
datapwa; adv. kahit paano
human /HYU-man/ n. tao;
adj. makatao, tauhan
humble /HAM-bol/ adj. mapa-
kumbaba, mababa; v. hamakin
hundred /HAN-dred/ num.
sandaan
hunger /HAN-gor/ n. gutom;
v. gutumin
hungry /HAN-gri/ adj. na-
gugutom
hunt /hant/ v. hanapin; n.
hanap
hunter /HON-ter/ n. ma-
ngangalap

hurry /HOR-i/ v. dalasin,
 habulin, dali-daliin,
 kahog
hurt; hurt; hurt /hurt;
 hurt; hurt/ v. isaktan;
 sinaktan; nasaktan; n.
 saktan, sakit
husband /HAZ-band/ n.
 asawang lalaki
hut /hat/ n. kubo, kamalig,
 barung-barong
I /ay/ prn. ako
ice /ays/ n. yelo
ice-cream /ays-KRIM/ n.
 surbetes
icy /AY-si/ adj. mayelo
idea /ay-DI-a/ n. isip,
 palagay, munukala
ideal /ay-DI-al/ adj.
 uliran
idle /AY-dol/ adj. tamad,
 "nakastan-by"
idleness /AY-dol-nas/ n.
 katamaran
if /if/ conj. kung

ill /il/ adj. may sakit
illness /IL-nas/ n. sakit
imaginary /e-MAY-jen-er-i/
 adj. sa guni-guni
imagination /e-may-jen-E-
 syan/ n. guni-guni
imagine /i-MAY-jen/ v.
 guni-gunihin
imitate /IM-a-tet/ v.
 gayahin
imitation /im-a-TE-syan/
 n. gagad, gaya
immediate /a-MI-di-ayt/
 adj. pagdaka
immediately /a-MI-di-ayt-
 li/ adv. agad, kapagdaka
immense /i-MENS/ adj.
 malaki-laki
importance /em-POR-tans/
 n. kahalagahan
important /em-POR-tant/
 adj. mahalaga
improve /em-PRUV/ v. napag-
 bago
improvement /em-PRUV-mant/
 n. pagkakabago

in /in/ prep. sa
in a week /in a WIK/ ex. sa
  loob ng isang linggo
inch /inch/ n. dali
include /en-KLUD/ v. ilakip,
  isali
inconvenience /en-kan-VIN-
  yans/ n. kaabalahan; v.
  makaaabala
inconvenient /en-kan-VIN-
  yant/ adj. naabala
incorrect /in-kor-EKT/ adj.
  di-tama, mali
increase /en-KRIS/ v. dagdagan, damihan, palakhin;
  n. dagdag
indeed /en-DID/ adv. talaga,
  siyanga
independence /en-di-PAYN-
  dans/ n. kasarinlan, kalayaan
independent /en-di-PAYN-
  dant/ adj. sarilining,
  malaya

indoors /en-DORZ/ adv. sa
loob ng bahay
industrial /en-DAS-tri-al/
adj. panghanapbuhay,
pangalalang
industry /IN-das-tri/ n.
kalalang
inexpensive /in-eks-PEN-
siv/ adj. di-mahal, mura
infect /in-FAYKT/ v. manghawa
influence /IN-flu-ans/ n.
bisa, palakasan; v. pa-
sunurin
influential /in-flu-EN-
syal/ adj. malakas magpa-
sunod
inform /en-FORM/ v. pa-
alam, bigay-alam
information /in-for-ME-syan/
n. kaalaman
ink /ink/ n. tinta
inn /in/ n. bahay-pahingahan
inquire /en-KWAYR/ v. usisain, tanungin, usigin

inquiry /IN-kwa-ri/ n. pagsiyasat, usig
insect /IN-sekt/ n. kulisap
inside /in-SAYD/ n. loob,
kalooban; adv. sa loob
instant /IN-stant/ n. kisap-
mata, takna
instantly /IN-stant-li/
adv. kapagdaka
instead /en-STED/ adv. sa
halip
instrument /IN-stru-mant/
n. instrumento
insult /IN-salt/ n. mina-
mura; v. murahin
insurance /en-SHUR-ans/ n.
seguro
intend /in-TEND/ v. bina-
balak, sadyain
intention /in-TEN-syan/ n.
balak
interest /IN-ta-rest/ n.
hilig, tubo, patong
interesting /IN-tres-teng/
adj. kaaga-agaya

interfere /en-tor-FIR/
v. pakialamin
interference /in-tor-FIR-
ans/ n. himasok, pakialam
international /in-tor-NAYS-
yan-al/ adj. pandaigdig,
sansinukubin
interrupt /in-tor-APT/ v.
sumabad, pinahinto
into /in-TU/ prep. sa, sa
loob ng
introduce /en-tro-DUS/ v.
pinakilala
introduction /in-tro-DAK-
syan/ n. pagpapakilala,
pagbungad
invent /en-VENT/ v. mag-
imbento
invention /in-VEN-syan/
n. imbento
inventor /in-VEN-tor/ n.
imbentor
invitation /en-vi-TE-syan/
n. anyaya
invite /in-VAYT/ v. kumbidahin, inanyayahan

inward /IN-ward/ adj. ka-
 looban
inwards /IN-wardz/ adv. sa
 kalooban
iron /AY-orn/ n. bakal,
 plantsa; adj. gawang bakal;
 v. plantsahin, pirinsahin
irregular /i-REG-u-lor/ adj.
 di-pantay, baku-bako,
 aliwaswas
is /iz/ v. ay
island /AY-lond/ n. pulo
it /it/ prn. ito
its /its/ adj. na ito, ng
 ito
itself /it-SELF/ prn. itong
 sarili, sarili niya
January /JAYN-yu-er-i/ n.
 Enero
jar /jar/ n. banga
jaw /joa/ n. sihang; v.
 ngawngaw
jealous /JA-los/ adj. panibugho
jewel /JIW-al/ n. batong
 brilyante

jewelry /JIW-al-ri/ n.
 alahas, hiyas
join /joen/ v. umanib
joint /joent/ n. kasu-
 kasuan; adj. magkaanib
joke /jok/ n. biro; v. magbiro
journey /JUR-ni/ n. paglalakbay; lakbayin
joy /joy/ n. galak
judge /jaj/ n. huwis, hukom
judgment /JAJ-mant/ n. ka-
 pasyahan, bait
juice /jus/ n. katas
July /Ju-LAY/ n. Hulyo
jump /jamp/ v. lundagin; n.
 lundag, lukso, talon
June /Jun/ n. Hunyo
just /jast/ adj. husto
justice /JAS-tas/ n. katarungan
justly /JAST-li/ adv. maka-
 tarungan
keep; kept; kept /kip; kept;
 kept/ v. itago; tinago;
 naitago

keep talking /kip TAO-keng/
v. walang tigil sa kasa-
salita
keeper /KI-por/ n. tagapag-
tago, katiwala
key /ki/ n. susi
kick /kayk/ v. sipain; n.
sipa
kill /kil/ v. patayin
kind /kaynd/ n. klase, uri
kindly /KAYND-li/ adj. mabait
kindness /KAYND-nas/ n.
kabaitan
king /king/ n. hari
kingdom /KING-dam/ n. ka-
harian, lupain
kiss /kes/ v. halikan; n.
halik
kitchen /KI-chan/ n. kusina,
batalan, lutuan
knee /ni/ n. tuhod
kneel; knelt; knelt /nil;
nelt; nelt/ v. luhod; lu-
muhod; nakaluhod

knife /nayf/ n. kutsilyo

knock /nak/ v. tuktukin, katukin; n. tuktok, katok

knot /nat/ n. buhol, tali;
v. ibuhol, talian

know; knew; known /no; nu;
non/ v. alam; nalaman;
alam na

knowledge /NA-lej/ n. karunungan, dunong, muwang

lack /layk/ v. magkulang,
kulangin; n. kulang

ladder /LAY-dor/ n. akyatan,
hagdan

lady /LE-di/ n. ale, babae

lake /lek/ n. lawa

lamp /laymp/ n. ilawan,
tanglaw

land /laynd/ n. lupa, bayan,
lupain; v. padpad, lumapag

landlord /LAYND-lord/ n.
kasero

language /LAYN-gwej/ n.
wika, kawikaan

large /larj/ adj. malaki

largely /LARJ-li/ adv. halos
last /layst/ adv. hulihan;
 adj. **pinakahuli**, kulalat;
 v. matira
late /let/ adv. nahuli; adj.
 panghuli
lately /LET-li/ adv. sa kasalukuyan
later /LE-tar/ adv. saka na
latter /LAY-tor/ adj. itong
 huli
laugh /laef/ **v.** tawa, halakhakan
laughter /LAEF-tor/ n. tawa,
 halakhak
law /loa/ n. batas
lawyer /LO-yer/ n. manananggol
lay; laid; laid /le; led;
 led/ v. **ibinaba**; naibaba;
 nababa
lazy /LE-zi/ adj. tamad
lead /layd/ n. tingga
lead; led; led /lid; layd;
 layd/ **v.** pasimuno; nagpasimuno; nagpasimuno

leader /LI-dor/ n. pinuno
leadership /LI-der-ship/ n.
 pangkalahatan patnugot
leading /LI-deng/ adj. na-
 ngunguna
leaf /lif/ n. dahon; pl.,
 mga dahon
leak /lik/ n. tulo, butas;
 v. tumulo
lean; leaned; leaned /lin;
 lind; lind/ v. magsandal;
 sumandal; nagsandal
learn; learned; learned
 /lern; lernd; lernd/ v. matutuhan; natuto; natuto
learning /LUR-neng/ n. matutuhan
least /list/ adj. pinaka;
 n. pinakakaunti
leather /LE-thor/ n. balat,
 katad; adj. balat na
leave; left; left /liv;
 left; left/ v. alis;
 umalis; naalis
left /left/ adv. kaliwa;
 adj. natira

leg /leg/ n. binti
lend; lent; lent /lend; lent;
 lent/ v. pautang; pinau-
 tang; nagpautang
length /length/ n. haba
less /les/ adj. kulang;
 adv. kulang pa
lessen /LES-an/ v. bawasan
lesson /LES-an/ n. aral
lest /lest/ conj. para hindi
let; let; let /let; let; let/
 v. hayaan; hinayaan; na-
 hayaan
letter /LAY-tar/ n. sulat,
 liham, titik
level /LAY-val/ adj. patag;
 n. palapag; v. pantayin
library /LAY-brer-i/ n.
 aklatan
lid /lid/ n. takip, suklob
lie; lay; lain /lay; le;
 len/ v. higa; humiga;
 nahiga
lie; lied; lied /lay; layd;
 layd/ v. sinungaling; nag-
 sinungaling; nagsinunga-
 ling; n. kasinungalingan

life /layf/ n. buhay
lift /lift/ v. buhatin, alsahin
light; lit; lit /layt; lit;
 lit/ v. sindihan; sinindi-
 han; nasindihan; n. ilaw;
 adj. magaan
lightly /LAYT-li/ adv.
 gaanan
like /layk/ v. gusto, ibigin; n. gusto, ibig; adj.
 kapilas; prep. kagaya
likely /LAYK-li/ adv., adj.
 malamang, siguro
limb /lim/ n. sanga
limit /LI-met/ n. takda,
 taning; v. taningan
limitation /li-ma-TE-syan/
 n. taning, takda
line /layn/ n. guhit, hanay,
 taludtod; v. pumila
liner /LAY-nor/ n. bapor
lip /lep/ n. labi; pl., mga
 labi

liquid /LI-kwid/ n. likido,
danum; adj. malapuyot,
likido
list /list/ n. listahan;
v. listahin
listen /LIS-en/ v. makinig,
pinakinggan
literary /LI-tor-er-i/ adj.
pampanitikan
literature /LI-tor-a-chur/
n. panitikan
little /LI-tol/ adj. maliit;
adv. maliit lang
live /liev/ v. mamuhay,
nakatira
lives /layvz/ n. pl. mga
buhay
living /LI-veng/ adj. nabubuhay; n. hanapbuhay, pag-
kabuhay
load /lod/ n. hakot; v. hakutin
loaf /lof/ n. pan de unan;
pl. mga pandisal
loan /lon/ v. pahiram; n.
hiram, utang

local /LO-kal/ adj. pampook
lock /lak/ n. kandado; v.
  susian
lodging /LAJ-eng/ n. tirahan
log /laog/ n. troso
lonely /LON-li/ adj. ma-
  lumbay
long /laong/ adj. mahaba;
  v. ilunghati
look /luok/ v. tingnan, si-
  patin; n. tingin
look after /luok AYF-tor/
  v. kupkupin, damayan
look for /LUOK for/ v. hanapin, hagilapin
look forward to /luok FOR-
  ward tu/ v. abangan, nag-
  aantay, maghintay
loose /lus/ adj. maluwag,
  maluwang, tanggal, hagpos
loosen /LU-sen/ v. luwagan
lord /lord/ n. Poon, lakan,
  maginoo; v. magamuhan
lose; lost; lost /luz; laost;
  laost/ v. iwala; nawala;
  nawala

lot /lat/ n. lote
lots of /LATS aov/ adv. marami ng, karami-rami
loud /lawd/ adj. maingay
loudly /LAWD-li/ adv. napalakas
love /lav/ n. pagibig; v. pakamahalin, sintahin
lovely /LAV-li/ adj. kahalihalina
lover /LAV-or/ n. kasintahan, magkalaguyo
low /lo/ adj. mababa; adv. baba
lower /LO-war/ adj. kababaang; v. ibaba
loyal /LOY-al/ adj. timtiman
loyalty /LOY-al-ti/ n. katapatan
lubricant /LUB-ri-kant/ n. langisan
luck /loak/ n. suwerte
lucky /LOAK-i/ adj. masuwerte, mapalad
luggage /LAG-ej/ n. bagahe, mga dala

lump /lamp/ n. limpak, kim-
 pal; v. limpak-limpak
lunch /lanch/ n. tanghalian;
 v. mananghali
lung /lang/ n. baga; pl. mga
 baga
machine /ma-SHIN/ n. makina
machinery /ma-SHIN-or-i/ n.
 mga makina, makinarya
mad /mayd/ adj. nagalit,
 baliw, haling
mail /mel/ n. sulat, mga sulat; v. ihulog
main /men/ adj. pangunahing
mainly /MEN-li/ adv. halos
make; made; made /mek; med;
 med/ v. yariin; niyari;
 nayari; n. gawa
maker /ME-kor/ n. tigagawa
male /mel/ adj. panlalaki;
 n. lalaki
man /maen/ n. lalaki; pl.
 mga lalaki
manage /MAEN-ej/ v. mangasiwa

management /MAEN-ej-mant/
n. pangangasiwa
manager /MAEN-a-jor/ n. katiwala, tagapangasiwa
manhood /MAEN-hued/ n. ka-
lalakihan
mankind /maen-KAYND/ n. sankatauhan
manner /MAEN-or/ n. asal
manufacture /maen-yu-FAYK-
chur/ v. yarian
manufacturer /maen-yu-FAYK-
chur-or/ n. tagapagyari
many /ME-ni/ adj. marami
map /maep/ n. mapa; v. ma-
pahin
March /March/ n. Marso
march /march/ v. magmartsa;
n. martsa
mark /mark/ n. guhit, marka,
tanda; v. markahan, ta-
takan, galusan
market /MAR-ket/ n. pa-
lengke; v. magtinda
marriage /MER-ij/ n. kasal

marry /ME-ri/ v. pakasal
mass /maes/ n. bugat, misa;
 v. magipon-ipon
master /MAES-tor/ n. amo,
 panginoon; v. amuin
masterpiece /MAES-tor-pis/
 n. pambato, obra muestra
mat /maet/ n. banig, kus-
 kusan, bangkuwang; v.
 banigin
match /maech/ n. kaparis,
 posporo, pansindi; v.
 parisan
material /ma-TIR-i-al/ n.
 sangkap; adj. panglupa
matter /MAE-tor/ v. may kuwenta; n. butang
May /May/ n. Mayo
may /may/ v. maka, maaaring
maybe /MAY-bi/ adv. yata,
 marahil
me /mi/ prn. ko, akin
meal /MI-al/ n. pagkain,
 kakanin

mean; meant; meant /min;
 ment; ment/ v. ibig sabihin; naibig sabihin; naibig sabihin; n. tamtaman;
 adj. imbi, marungis, tam-
 tamang
meaning /MI-neng/ n. ibig
 sabihin, kahulugan
meantime /MIN-taym/ adv.
 samantala, habang
meanwhile /MIN-hwayl/ adv.
 samantala, habang
measure /MEZ-ur/ v. sukatan,
 takalan, dangkalin; n.
 sukat, takal
meat /mit/ n. karne
mechanical /mi-KAYN-e-kol/
 adj. mekaniko, pangmakina
medical /MED-i-kol/ adj.
 panggamutan
medicine /MED-i-son/ n.
 gamot
meet; met; met /mit; met;
 met/ v. magtagpo; tinagpo;
 nagtagpo; n. tagpuan

meeting /MIT-eng/ n. pulong
melt /melt/ v. lusawin
member /MEM-bor/ n. kasapi,
  kagawad
membership /MEM-bor-ship/
  n. pagkakaanib
memorial /me-MOR-i-al/ n.
  bantayog
memory /MEM-or-i/ n. gunita,
  alaala
mend /mend/ v. sulsihan;
  n. sulsi
mention /MEN-syan/ v. banggitin; n. banggit
merchant /MER-chant/ n.
  negosyante
mercy /MER-si/ n. biyaya,
  awa
mere /mir/ adj. lamang,
  iyon lang
merely /MIR-li/ adv. basta
merry /MER-i/ adj. masaya
mess /mes/ n. lamas, gulo;
  v. lamasin, guluhin
message /MES-ij/ n. mensahe

messenger /MES-an-jer/ n.
 mensahero
metal /ME-tal/ n. bakal
middle /MI-dol/ n. gitna;
 adj. gitnaan
middle-aged /mi-dol EJD/
 adj. katanghalian-gulang
middle class /mi-dol KLAYS/
 n. katamtamang klase
midnight /MID-nayt/ n. hatinggabi; adj. hatinggabian
midway /mid-WE/ n., adv.
 kalagitnaan
might /mayt/ v. baka; n.
 kapangyarihan, lakas
mighty /MAYT-i/ adj. ma-
 lakas; adv. napaka, ubod
mild /mayld/ adj. matabang
mile /mayl/ n. milya
milk /milk/ n. gatas; v.
 gatasan
mill /mil/ n. kiskisan; v.
 ikiskis
mind /maynd/ n. isip; v.
 intindihin

mine /mayn/ prn. aking; n.
 mina; v. minahin
miner /MAY-nor/ n. minero
mineral /MI-nor-al/ n. mineral; adj. minahan
minister /MI-nas-tor/ n.
 ministro, pastor; v. da-
 mayan
minute /MI-nat/ n. minuto,
 sandali
miserable /MI-sor-a-bol/
 adj. kawawa
misery /MI-sor-i/ n. pag-
 durusa
Miss /mis/ n., ref. binibini
miss /mis/ v. daplisan; n.
 daplis, paltik
mistake /mis-TEK/ n. kamalian, bisala; v. lisyain
misunderstanding /mis-an-
 dor-STAYN-deng/ n. di-
 pagkakaunawaan
mix /miks/ v. haluin; n.
 halungkap

mixture /MIKS-chur/ n. halungkap, halu-halo

model /MA-dol/ n. huwaran; v. huwarin

moderate /MA-dor-ayt/ adj. banayad; v. magtimpi

modern /MA-dorn/ adj. makabago

modest /MA-dest/ adj. mahinhin, mayumi, mabini

moment /MO-mant/ n. sandali

Monday /MAN-de/ n. Lunes

money /MA-ni/ n. pera, kuwarta, salapi

monkey /MAN-ki/ n. unggoy, tsonggo

month /manth/ n. buwan

monthly /MANTH-li/ adj. buwanan; adv. buwan-buwan

moon /mun/ n. buwan

moonlight /MUN-layt/ n. sikat ng buwan, sinag; v. lamayin

moral /MOR-al/ n. aral; adj. masanling

morality /mor-AYL-a-ti/ n.
 kasanlingan
more /mor/ adv. lalo; adj.
 higit
moreover /mor-O-var/ adv.
 pati
morning /MOR-neng/ n. umaga
most /most/ adj. pinaka;
 adv. sakdal; n. pinaka-
 marami
mostly /MOST-li/ adv. halos
mother /MA-thor/ n. ina
motion /MO-syan/ n. galaw,
 kilos, kibo; v. kawayan,
 magmungkahi
motor /MO-tar/ n. motor, da-
 gisog; v. magmotor
mountain /MAWN-tan/ n. bundok; adj. bulubundukin
mouse /maws/ n. bubuwit,
 daga; pl. "mga mabait"
mouth /mawth/ n. bibig
move /muv/ n. galaw, lipat;
 v. kilusin, galawin, lu-
 mipat

movement /MUV-mant/ n. kilos, kilusan, kumpas, kibo
much /mach/ adj., adv.
  marami
mud /mad/ n. putik, lusak
multiply /MOL-ta-play/ v.
  paramiin
murder /MAR-der/ n. pagpatay
  ng tao; v. pumatay ng tao
music /MU-zik/ n. tugtog
musical /MU-za-kol/ adj.
  tugtugin
musician /mu-ZI-syan/ n.
  musikero
must /mast/ v. kailangan;
  n. pangangailangan
my /may/ prn. aking, ko
myself /may-SELF/ prn.
  sarili ko
mysterious /mes-TIR-i-as/
  adj. mahiwaga
mystery /MIS-ta-ri/ n.
  hiwaga
nail /nel/ n. pako; v. pakuan

name /nem/ n. pangalan; v.
  pangalanan
namely /NEM-li/ adv. ala-
  laong baga
narrow /NE-ro/ adj. makipot,
  makitid; v. kitiran
nation /NE-syan/ n. bansa
national /NAE-syo-nal/ adj.
  pambansa; n. kababayan
native /NE-tiv/ adj. angkin,
  katutubo; n. taal
natural /NAY-chu-ral/ adj.
  likas, katutubo
naturally /NAYCH-ra-li/
  adv. siyempre
nature /NE-chur/ n. kali-
  kasan
near /nir/ adj. malapit;
  adv. lapit-lapit; v. su-
  mapit, lumapit, lapitan
nearly /NIR-li/ adv. munti
neat /nit/ adj. aliwalas,
  maayos
necessary /NE-ses-er-i/
  adj. kailangan

neck /nek/ n. leeg, liig
need /nid/ v. kailanganin;
  n. pagdadahop, pangangailangan
needle /NI-dol/ n. karayom
neglect /ni-GLEKT/ v. pabayaan; n. kapabayaan
neighbor /NE-bor/ n. kapitbahay
neighborhood /NE-bor-had/
  n. magkakapitbahay
neither /NI-thar/ prn.,
  adj., conj. ni
nephew /NEF-yu/ n. pamangkin
nest /nest/ n. pugad
net /net/ n. lambat; adj.
  sumang; v. ilambat
never /NE-var/ adv. di-
  kailanman
new /niw/ adj. bago
news /niwz/ n. balita
newspaper /NIWZ-pe-por/ n.
  pahayagan
next /nekst/ adj. susunod;
  adv. kasunod

nice /nays/ adj. mainam
night /nayt/ n. gabi
nine /nayn/ num. siyam
nineteen /nayn-TIN/ num.
 labinsiyam
ninety /NAYN-ti/ num. siyamnapu
noble /NO-bal/ adj. maharlika; n. senyor, senyora
nobody /NO-ba-di/ prn. walang tao; n. taong bale-
 wala
noise /noyz/ n. ingay
noisy /NOY-zi/ adj. maingay
none /nan/ prn., adv. wala,
 wala na
nonsense /NAN-sens/ n. kabululan, kalokohan
noon /nun/ n. tanghali
nor /nor/ conj. ni
north /north/ n., adv.
 hilaga
northern /NOR-thern/ adj.
 hilagang
northward /NORTH-ward/ adv.
 bandang hilaga

northwest /north-WEST/ adj.,
adv. hilagang-kanluran
nose /noz/ n. ilong; v. nubok, manman
not /nat/ adv. di, hindi
not a /nat E/ adv., ex. ni
isang, ni kapranting
note /not/ n. pasabi; v. i-
lista, tandaan
nothing /NA-theng/ n., adv.
wala
notice /NO-tes/ v. inuhin,
tandaan; n. paunawa, ba-
bala
noticeable /NO-tes-a-bol/
adj. halata, kapuna-puna
November /No-VEM-bar/ n.
Nobyembre
now /naw/ adv. ngayon
nowadays /NAW-a-dez/ adv.
sa kasalukuyan
nowhere /NO-hwer/ adv. wala
kahit saan
nude /nud/ adj. hubad, hubo
nuisance /NU-sans/ n. abala

number /NAM-ber/ n. bilang;
  v. bilangin
numerous /NU-mor-as/ adj.
  di-mabilang, marami
nurse /nors/ n. nars, yaya,
  mamay
oar /or/ n. pangaod
obedient /o-BID-i-ant/ adj.
  masunurin
obey /o-BE/ v. sundin, su-
  munod, talatuntunin
object /AB-jekt/ n. bagay,
  pakay; v. tumutol
objection /ab-JEK-syan/ n.
  tutol
observation /ab-sor-VE-syan/
  n. pagmasdan
observe /ab-ZURV/ v. masdan,
  magmasid
occasion /o-KE-syan/ n.
  pangyayari; v. yariin
occasional /o-KE-syan-al/
  adj. pangminsan
occasionally /o-KE-syan-a-
  li/ adv. paminsan-minsan

ocean /O-syan/ n. dagat
October /ak-TO-bor/ n.
 Oktubre
odd /ad/ adj. pambihira,
 gansal
of /av/ prep. ng, ni
off /aof/ adv. inalis
offend /o-FEND/ v. alipustain
offer /AW-for/ v. dulutan,
 alukin; n. dulot, alok
office /AW-fis/ n. tang-
 gapan
officer /AW-fi-sor/ n. pinuno, katiwala
official /o-FIS-yal/ adj.
 pampamahalaan; n. tauhan
often /AW-fen/ adv. madalas
oil /oyl/ n. langis; v.
 langisan
O.K., okay /o-KE/ adv. sige,
 okay lang; v. aprubahan
old /old/ adj. matanda, luma
old-fashioned /old FAE-
 syand/ adj. makaluma

omit /o-MIT/ v. makaligtaan
on /an/ prep. sa, na sa;
 adv. tuloy na
on to /AN tu/ ex. tuloy na
 tuloy
once /wans/ adv. minsanan;
 conj. kapag
one /wan/ num., prn. isa;
 adj. isang
only /ON-li/ adj., adv. lamang, lang; conj. subali't
open /O-pan/ v. buksan, buklatin; adj. bukas, buka
openly /O-pan-li/ adv. ha-
 yagan
operate /AP-or-et/ v. umandar, inopera
operation /ap-or-E-syan/ n.
 sakilos, pagpapalakad, pag-
 opera
opinion /o-PIN-yan/ n.
 palagay
opportunity /a-por-TUN-i-
 ti/ n. pagkakataon
oppose /a-POZ/ v. labanan

opposite /A-po-sit/ adj. tapatan, magkatapat; adv. baligtad

oppression /o-PRE-syan/ n. pagsiil, kaapihan

or /or/ conj. o

orange /OR-enj/ n. kahel; adj. salmon

order /OR-dar/ n. utos, ayos, tagubilin; v. inutos, tagubilinan, atasan

ordinary /OR-din-er-i/ adj. karaniwa

organ /OR-gan/ n. organo

organization /or-gayn-ay-ZE-syan/ n. kapisanan, samahan, katatagan

organize /OR-gayn-ayz/ v. ayusin, magtatag

origin /OR-a-jin/ n. pinagmulan

original /or-IJ-e-nal/ adj. unang-una, mulaang; n. orihinal

originally /o-RIJ-e-nal-i/ adv. sa una

ornament /OR-na-ment/ n.
pampaganda; v. gandahan
other /A-thar/ adj. iba;
prn. iyong iba
otherwise /A-thar-wayz/ adv.
kung hindi
ought /oat/ v. dapat
our /awr/ adj. nating, ating
out /awt/ adv. labas
out of /AWT av/ adv. labas
ng, naubos na
outbreak /AWT-brek/ n. sumiklab
outcome /AWT-kam/ n. kinalabasan
outdoors /awt-DORZ/ adj. sa
labas; n. labasan
outer /AW-tar/ adj. sa labasan
outlet /AWT-let/ n. labasan
outline /AWT-layn/ n. hugis,
balangkas, banghay; v. hugisan, balangkasin
outside /awt-SAYD/ adv. nasa
labas; n. labas; adj. sa
labasan

outward /AWT-ward/ adj.
 labas
over /O-var/ prep. sa ibabaw
 ng; adv. tapos na
overcome /o-var-KAM/ v. gapiin
overlook /o-var-LUOK/ v.
 pabayaan
owe /o/ v. may utang
own /on/ v. kani-kanila;
 adj. sarili
owner /O-nar/ n. may-ari
pack /payk/ v. magimpake;
 n. impake
package /PAYK-ej/ n. balutan
page /pej/ n. pahina
pail /pel/ n. balde
pain /pen/ n. hapdi, kirot;
 v. kumirot
painful /PEN-fal/ adj. masakit, mahapdi
paint /pent/ n. pinta; v.
 pintahan
painter /PEN-tar/ n. pintor
painting /PENT-eng/ n. kuwadro

pair /per/ n. pareha; v.
 dalawahin
pale /pel/ adj. maputla; v.
 putlain
pan /pan/ n. kawali
paper /PE-par/ n. papel;
 adj. gawang papel
pardon /PAR-dan/ n. patawad;
 v. patawarin
parent /PER-ant/ n. magu-
 lang; pl. mga magulang
park /park/ n. liwasan; v.
 maghinto ang kotse
part /part/ n. bahagi; v.
 humiwalay
particular /par-TIK-yu-lar/
 adj. maselang, busisi; n.
 pasikot-sikot
particularly /par-TIK-yu-
 lar-li/ adv. lalo na, mas
 pa
partly /PART-li/ adv. na-
 ngangalahati
party /PAR-ti/ n. pangkat,
 kapisanan, balangay

pass /paes/ n. lagpasan;
 v. lusot, daanan
passage /PAES-ej/ n. lusutan
passenger /PAES-an-jer/ n.
 pasahero
past /paest/ n. nakaraan;
 adv. lampas na
path /paeth/ n. landas
patience /PE-syans/ n. tiyaga
patient /PE-syant/ adj. matiyaga; n. may-sakit
patriotic /pe-tri-A-tik/
 adj. makabayan
pattern /PAE-tarn/ n. hulwaran, padron; v. hulmahin
pause /poaz/ n. patumangga,
 tigil; v. pigilin
pay; paid; paid /pe; ped;
 ped/ v. bayaran; binayaran; nagbayad; n. bayad
payment /PE-mant/ n. bayad
peace /pis/ n. kapayapaan
peaceful /PIS-fol/ adj.
 tahimik, mapayapa

pearl /perl/ n. perlas
peculiar /pi-KYUL-yar/ adj.
 pambihira
pen /pen/ n. pluma
pencil /PEN-sil/ n. lapis
penny /PEN-i/ n. sentimo,
 kusing
people /PI-pol/ n. mga tao
pepper /PAE-par/ n. paminta,
 sili
per /por/ prep. ayon kay
perfect /POR-fikt/ adj. mahusay, himpit; v. husayin,
 pagigihin
perfection /por-FEK-syan/
 n. kahusayan
perfectly /POR-fekt-li/
 adv. husto na
perform /per-FORM/ v. gu-
 manap
performance /per-FORM-ans/
 n. tanghalan, kaganapan
perhaps /por-HAEPS/ adv.
 baka, yata, marahil
permanent /POR-maen-ant/ adj.
 laging, pangmatagalan

permit /PAR-mit/ n. pahintulot, kapahintulutan; v. payagan, pahintulutan
person /PER-san/ n. tao
personal /PER-son-al/ adj.
masarili
personally /PER-son-al-i/
adv. makasarili
persuade /par-SWED/ v. ya-
yain, himukin, amukiin
pet /pet/ n. alaga; v. himasin
photograph /FO-to-grayf/ n.
litrato; v. ikunin ang litrato
pick /pik/ v. piliin; n.
pili
picture /PIK-chur/ n. la-
rawan; v. ilarawan
piece /pis/ n. bahagi; v.
bahagihin
pig /pig/ n. baboy
pile /payl/ n. salansan, tumpok; v. talaksan, magtumpok
pin /pin/ n. aspile; v. iduro

pinch /pinch/ v. ipitin, ku-
rutan; n. ipit, kurot
pink /pink/ adj. rosas
pint /paynt/ n. gatang
pipe /payp/ n. tubo, daluyan, kuwako; v. tubuhan
pity /PI-ti/ n. awa; v. ki-
naawa
place /ples/ n. lugar, pook;
v. ilagay
plain /plen/ adj. simple;
n. kapatagan
plan /plaen/ n. balak, munukala, banghay; v. balakin
plant /plaent/ n. halaman,
tanim; v. magtanim
plate /plet/ n. pinggan
play /ple/ v. maglaro, laruin; n. palabas
player /PLE-yar/ n. manlalaro
pleasant /PLE-sant/ adj. mainam, maginhawa
please /pliz/ v. bigyan ng
kasiyahan; ex. paki, nga

pleasure /PLE-sur/ n. li-
bangan
plenty /PLEN-ti/ n. sagana;
adv. masaganang
plough /plaw/ n. araro; v.
araruhin
plural /PLUR-al/ n. karamihan; adj. mga
pocket /PAK-et/ n. bolsa,
lukbutan; v. pamumulsa
pocketbook /PAK-et-buk/ n.
kalupi
poet /PO-at/ n. makata
point /poynt/ n. punto, gat-
la; v. ituro
poison /POY-san/ n. lason,
kamandag; v. lasunin
police /po-LIS/ n. pulis
policeman /po-LIS-man/ n.
pulis, hagad
polish /PAL-esh/ n. pakintab; v. pakintabin
polite /po-LAYT/ adj. mahinhin

political /po-LIT-i-kal/
 adj. pangpulitika
politics /PAL-a-tiks/ n.
 pulitika
pool /pul/ n. languyan, palaisdaan; v. pagsama-
 samahin
poor /pur/ adj. madusa, kawawa, dahop, maralita,
 hirap-na-hirap
popular /PAP-yu-ler/ adj.
 tanyag
popularity /pap-yu-LER-a-ti/
 n. katanyagan
population /pap-yu-LE-syan/
 n. santauhan
position /po-ZI-syan/ n. katayuan, puwesto; v. ilagay
possess /po-ZES/ v. kamtan,
 taglay, magdala
possession /po-ZES-yan/ n.
 pagaari
possibility /pas-a-BIL-a-ti/
 n. kapuwedehan
possible /PAS-a-bol/ adj.
 maaari, puwede, ubra

possibly /PAS-a-bli/ adv.
 kung sa bagay
post /post/ n. haligi; v.
 ihulog
postal /POS-tal/ adj. pang-
 koreo
post office /POST aw-fis/
 n. koreo
postpone /post-PON/ v.
 iliban
pot /pat/ n. palayok
pound /pawnd/ n. libra; v.
 pitpitin, dagukan
pour /por/ v. ibuhos
poverty /PA-var-ti/ n. karalitaan, kawalan
powder /PAW-der/ n. pulbos
power /PAW-ar/ n. kapang-
 yarihan, lambal; v. pa-
 andarin
powerful /PAW-ar-fol/ adj.
 malakas
practical /PRAYK-ti-kal/
 adj. masinop

practically /PRAYK-te-kli/
adv. makasinop, halos
practice /PRAYK-tes/ n. pag-
sasanay, kalakaran; v. sanayin
praise /prez/ n. puri; v.
purihin
pray /pre/ v. magdasal
prayer /PRE-ar/ n. dasal,
dalangin, panalangin
preach /prich/ v. mangaral
preacher /PRI-char/ n. ma-
ngangaral
precious /PRAY-syas/ adj.
mahalaga, masinta
prefer /pri-FER/ v. mas gusto
prejudice /PRAY-ju-des/ n.
laban sa loob; v. siniraan
preparation /pray-par-E-
syan/ n. paghahanda
prepare /pri-PER/ v. ihanda
presence /PRAY-sens/ n. pag-
dalo
present /PRAY-sent/ adj.
nandito; n. rigalo, han-
dog; v. magtanghal

preserve /pri-SERV/ v. imbakin

president /PRES-a-dent/ n. pangulo

presidential /prays-i-DENsyal/ adj. panguluhan

press /pres/ n. diin, mamamahayag; v. pirinsahin, pisilin, diinan

pressure /PRES-yur/ n. diin, pagdiin

pretend /pri-TAYND/ v. magmaang-maangan

pretty /PRE-ti/ adj. marikit; adv. medyo

prevent /pri-VENT/ v. hadlangan

price /prays/ n. halaga, presyo; v. halagahan

pride /prayd/ n. pagmataas

priest /prist/ n. pare, kura

print /print/ n. limbag; v. limbagin

prison /PRI-san/ n. bilangguan

prisoner /PRI-san-er/ n. bilanggo, bihag
private /PRAY-vat/ adj. sa-
rilinan, panarili
prize /prayz/ n. gantimpala;
v. gantimpalaan
probability /pra-ba-BIL-a-
ti/ n. kalagmitan
probably /PRA-ba-bli/ adv.
malamang
problem /PRAB-lum/ n. suliranin, problema
process /PRA-ses/ n. paraan;
v. inayos
produce /pro-DUS/ v. luwal,
yariin
product /PRA-dakt/ n. yari,
lalang
production /pro-DAK-syan/
n. dagsa, pangangalalang
profession /pro-FES-yan/
n. panungkulan
professional /pro-FES-yo-
nal/ adj. panungkulin; n.
manunungkulan

profit /PRA-fit/ n. kita, tubo, pakinabang; v. kitain,
pakinabangan
program /PRO-gram/ n. palabas, palatuntunan; v. pa-
labasin
progress /PRA-gres/ n. kaunlaran, pagunlad
promise /PRA-mes/ v. pangakuan; n. pangako
prompt /prampt/ adj. ma-
agap; v. manunsol
pronounce /pro-NAWNS/ v.
bigkasin
proof /pruf/ n. katibayan
proper /PRA-par/ adj. angkop
properly /PRA-por-li/ adv.
mahinusay
property /PRA-por-ti/ n.
pagaari, kaangkinan
proposal /pro-POS-al/ n.
panukala, alok
propose /pro-POZ/ v. alukin
protect /pro-TEKT/ v. mai-
pagsanggalang, lukuban

protection /pro-TEK-syan/
n. kupkop, pagkalinga,
kandili
proud /prawd/ adj. palalo,
mapagmataas
prove /pruv/ v. patunayan
provide /pro-VAYD/ v. an-
dukhain
provide for /pro-VAYD for/
v. sustentuhan
public /PAB-lik/ n. madla;
adj. pangmadla
pull /pul/ v. hilahin, ba-
takin, dukutin
pump /pamp/ n. pambomba;
v. bombahin
punish /PAN-esh/ v. parusa-
han
punishment /PAN-esh-mant/
n. parusa
pupil /PYU-pal/ n. inaaralan, tinuturuan
puppet /PAP-et/ n. tau-
tauhan

purchase /POR-chas/ v. bilhin; n. pinamili
pure /pyur/ adj. dalisay,
lantay, payak
purely /PYUR-li/ adv. wa-
lang halo
purpose /POR-pas/ n. sadya
push /posh/ v. itulak; n.
tulak
put; put; put /put; put; put/
v. ilagay; nailagay; nag-
lagay
puzzle /PAZ-ol/ n. bugtong
qualified /KWAL-a-fayd/
adj. mga tapos na
quality /KWAL-a-ti/ n. uri,
katampatan
quantity /KWAN-ta-ti/ n.
dami
quarrel /KWAR-el/ v. bangay-
in, awayin; n. away, sigalot, bangay
quarter /KWAR-tar/ n. beynte
singko; v. patirahin
queen /kwin/ n. reyna

question /KWES-chan/ n.
 tanong; v. tanungin
quick /kwik/ adj. madali,
 maliksi
quickly /KWIK-li/ adv. dali-
 dali
quiet /KWAY-at/ adj. tahimik, walang kibo; n. katahimikan
quietly /KWAY-at-li/ adv.
 matahimik
quite /kwayt/ adv. napaka,
 ubod
race /res/ n. karera, lahi;
 v. magkarera
radio /RE-di-o/ n. diglap
rail /rel/ n. riles
railing /REL-eng/ n. beranda
railroad /REL-rod/ n. riles,
 daambakal
railway /REL-we/ n. riles,
 daambakal
rain /ren/ n. ulan; v. umulan
raincoat /REN-kot/ n. kapote

raise /rez/ n. pagdagdag;
  v. alsahin, dagdagan, itaas
rank /raynk/ n. ranggo; v.
  ranguhin
rapid /RAE-pid/ adj. mabilis
rapidly /RAE-pid-li/ adv.
  kabilisan
rare /rer/ adj. bihira
rarely /RER-li/ adv. di-
  panay, pambihira
rat /raet/ n. daga
rate /ret/ n. lubig, antas,
  palit, bilis; v. antasin
rather /RAE-thar/ adv. mas
  gusto, medyo
raw /roa/ adj. hilaw
ray /re/ n. silahis
razor blade /RE-zor bled/
  n. labaha, pang-ahit
reach /rich/ v. abutan, datnin; n. pagabot
read; read; read /rid; red;
  red/ v. basahin; bumasa;
  nagbasa
reader /RI-dor/ n. tagabasa,
  babasahin, katon

ready /RE-di/ adj., adv.
 handa; v. ihanda
real /ril/ adj. tunay
reality /ri-AEL-a-ti/ n.
 katunayan
realize /RI-a-layz/ v. ma-
 tatap, damahin
really /RI-li/ adv. nga,
 talaga, siyanga
reason /RI-san/ n. katuwiran, dahilan, matwid; v. mangatuwiran
reasonable /RIZ-na-bol/
 adj. makatuwiran
receipt /ri-SIT/ n. resibo
receive /ri-SIV/ v. tanggapin
recent /RI-sant/ adj. bago
reckless /REK-las/ adj. ma-
 gaso
recognition /re-kog-NIS-yan/
 n. pagkakakilala
recognize /RE-kog-nayz/ v.
 namukhaan
recommend /re-ko-MAEND/
 v. tagubilinan

record /RE-kord/ n. talaan,
 plaka; v. itala
red /raed/ adj. mapula; n.
 pula
Red Cross /Raed KRAS/ n.
 Kurus na Pula
reduce /ri-DUS/ v. bawasan
reduction /ri-DAK-syan/ n.
 bawas, kabawasan
refer /ri-FER/ v. ipababaha-
 la, tukuyin, itukoy
reference /RAE-far-ens/ n.
 pagtukoy, pagpapabahala
reflect /ri-FLEKT/ v. nuy-
 nuyin, pagbulay-bulayin
reflection /ri-FLEK-syan/
 n. pagbubulay-bulay
refresh /ri-FRESH/ v. magpalamig
refusal /ri-FYU-sal/ n.
 tanggihan
refuse /ri-FYUZ/ v. tumanggi, ipagkait; n. yamutmot
regard /ri-GARD/ v. pakundangan; n. taros

regardless /ri-GARD-las/
 adv. maski na; adj. pabaya
regret /ri-GRET/ n. sisi;
 v. magsisi
regular /REG-yu-lar/ adj.
 regular
regularly /REG-yu-lar-li/
 adv. laging gawi
rejoice /ri-JOYS/ v. matuwa
relate /ri-LET/ v. mag-ulat,
 dalahirain
related /ri-LET-ad/ adj. kaugnay
relation /ri-LE-syan/ n. kaugnayan
relative /REL-a-tiv/ n. kamaganak; adj. pansamantala
relief /ri-LIF/ n. kagin-
 hawahan
relieve /ri-LIV/ v. relyebo
religion /ri-LIJ-an/ n.
 agamahan
religious /ri-LIJ-as/ adj.
 madasalin
remain /ri-MEN/ v. manatili

remark /ri-MARK/ n. tugon;
v. tugunin
remedy /REM-a-di/ n. remed-
yo; v. remedyuhin
remember /ri-MEM-bar/ v. a-
lalahanin, tandaan, guni-
tain
remind /ri-MAYND/ v. paalala
repair /ri-PER/ v. kumpunihin; n. kumpusisyon, pag-
papaayos
repeat /ri-PIT/ v. ulitin
replace /ri-PLES/ v. kapalitan
reply /ri-PLAY/ v. tugunin;
n. tugon
report /ri-PORT/ n. ulat;
v. iulat, isuplung
reporter /ri-POR-tar/ n.
mamamahayag
represent /rep-ri-SENT/ v.
katawanin
representative /rep-ri-SEN-
ta-tiv/ adj. sugo; n. kinatawan

reproduce /ri-pro-DUS/ v.
 doblihin
republic /ri-PAB-lik/ n.
 republika
reputation /re-pyu-TE-syan/
 n. karangalan
request /ri-KWEST/ v. maki-
 usap, hingi; n. luhog
rescue /RES-kyu/ v. iligtas,
 saklolohan; n. pagligtas
reserve /ri-SERV/ v. imbakin; n. imbak, pataan
resign /ri-ZAYN/ v. nagbi-
 tiw ng puwesto
resist /ri-SIST/ v. aklas
resistance /ri-SIS-tans/
 n. aklasan
responsibility /res-pans-a-
 BIL-a-ti/ n. pananagutan
responsible /res-PANS-a-
 bol/ adj. may pananagutan,
 maasa
rest /rest/ n. pahinga; v.
 pahingahin, humpayan
restaurant /RES-trant/ n.
 karihan

restroom /REST-rum/ n. palikuran, banyo
result /ri-SALT/ n. bunga,
kinahinatnan; v. kinalab-
asan
retire /ri-TAYR/ v. magre-
tiro
retirement /ri-TAYR-mant/
n. retiro
return /ri-TURN/ v. ibalik,
isauli; n. pagbalik
revenge /ri-VAENJ/ n. hi-
ganti; v. maghiganti
review /ri-VIW/ v. balik-
aralin; n. balik-aral
reward /ri-WARD/ n. gantimpala
rice /rays/ n. kanin, bigas
rich /rich/ adj. mayaman
rid; rid; ridded /rid; rid;
RID-ad/ v. alisin; inia-
lis; inalisan
ride; rode; ridden /rayd;
rod; RID-an/ v. sakay, sumakay; nakasakay

right /rayt/ adj. tama, kanan; adv. sa kanan; n. karapatan, mano; v. wastuin
rightly /RAYT-li/ adv. na
husto, na dapat
ring; rang; rung /ring;
raeng; rang/ v. kuling; kumuliling; kumuliling; n.
singsing; n. kuliling
ripe /rayp/ adj. hinog
ripen /RAYP-an/ v. hinugin
rise; rose; risen /rayz; roz;
RIZ-an/ v. alsahin; umalsa;
nagalsa; n. alsa
risk /risk/ n. pusta; v. pumusta
rival /RAY-val/ n. kalaban;
v. kalabanin
river /RIV-ar/ n. ilog
road /rod/ n. daan
roar /ror/ n. ungal; v. u-
mungol
roast beef /rost BIF/ n.
asado
rob /rab/ v. nakawin

rock /rak/ n. bato; v. u-
  goyin
rod /rad/ n. bingwit, ping-
  ga
roll /rol/ v. ikirin, lulunin; n. ikid
roof /ruf/ n. bubungan
room /rum/ n. silid
root /rut/ n. ugat; v. kurakot
rope /rop/ n. lubid; v. lu-
  birin
rough /raf/ adj. magasgas,
  baku-bako
roughly /RAF-li/ adv. mahig-
  pitan, mga
round /rawnd/ adj. mabilog;
  prep. maligid; n. sakay;
  v. bilugin
row /ro/ n. hanay, gaod;
  v. gumaod
royal /ROY-al/ adj. hari-
  harian
rub /rab/ v. hilutin, hagurin, kuskusin; n. hagod

rubber /RO-bar/ n. goma
rude /rud/ adj. bastos
rug /rag/ n. alpombra
ruin /RU-an/ v. gibain; n.
  giba, panganyaya
rule /rul/ n. tuntunin, sakop; v. sakupin
ruler /RU-lor/ n. panukat
run; ran; run /ran; raen;
  ran/ v. takbo; tumakbo;
  nagtakbo; n. takbuhan
rush /rash/ v. ugaga, kahog;
  n. hugos
rust /rast/ n. kalawang; v.
  kalawangin
sacred /SEK-rad/ adj. banal
sacrifice /SAEK-ri-fays/ v.
  pagtiisan; n. pagpapaka-
  sakit
sad /saed/ adj. malungkot,
  mapanglaw
saddle /SAE-dol/ v. sing-
  kawan
safe /sef/ adj. ligtas; n.
  kahadiyero

safety /SEF-ti/ n. ikali-
ligtas, kaligtasan
sail /sel/ n. layag; v. mag-
layag
sailor /SE-lor/ n. marino
sake /sek/ n. alang-alang
salary /SAE-la-ri/ n. pa-
sahod, suweldo
sale /sel/ n. paninda, pinagbilhan
salesman /SELS-man/ n. man-
lalako
salt /salt/ n. asin; v. a-
sinan
salty /SAL-ti/ adj. maalat
same /sem/ adj. magkaparis,
pareho
sample /SAEM-pol/ n. pasubok
sand /saend/ n. buhangin
satisfaction /sae-tis-FAEK-
syan/ n. kasiyahan
satisfactory /sae-tis-FAEK-
to-ri/ adj. kasiya
satisfy /SAE-tis-fay/ v.
bigyan ng kasiyahan

Saturday /SAE-tur-de/ n.
 Sabado
sauce /saws/ n. sarsa
sausage /SAW-sej/ n. longun-
 isa
save /sev/ v. iligtas, impukin
saw; sawed; sawn /saw; sawd;
 sawn/ v. lagariin; nila-
 gari; nilagari; n. lagari
say; said; said /se; saed;
 saed/ v. sabihin; sinabi;
 nagsabi
scale /skel/ n. timbangan;
 v. akyatin
scar /skar/ n. peklat
scarce /skers/ adj. bihira
scarcely /SKERS-li/ adv. bahagya
scatter /SKAET-or/ v. ikalat
scene /sin/ n. tanawin
scent /saent/ n. sanyo,
 bango; v. amuyin
school /skul/ n. paaralan;
 adj. pampaaralan

science /SAY-ans/ n. agham
scientific /say-an-TIF-ik/
 adj. pangkaaghaman
scientist /SAY-an-tist/ n.
 siyentipiko
scissors /SIS-ors/ n. gunting
scold /skold/ v. ngawngaw
scorn /skorn/ n. minamata;
 v. matahin, alimurahin
scrape /skrep/ v. kalkal,
 kutkutin
scratch /skraetch/ v. kamutin, kalmutin; n. kamot;
 galos, gasgas
screen /skrin/ n. tabing;
 v. tabingan, salain
screw /skriw/ n. turnilyo;
 v. turnilyuhin
sea /si/ n. dagat
seaman /SI-man/ n. marino
search /surch/ v. halung-
 katin, hanapin, hagilapin;
 n. hanap, rikisa
seaside /SI-sayd/ n. tabing
 dagat, dalampasigan

season /SI-son/ n. panahon;
  v. isahog
seat /sit/ n. upuan; v. pa-
  upuin
second /SE-kand/ adj. pangalawa, ikalawa; n. saglit;
  v. alalayan
secondly /SE-kand-li/ adv.
  pangalawahan
secret /SI-kraet/ n. lihim;
  adj. malihim
secretary /SAEK-ra-te-ri/
  n. kalihim
see; saw; seen /si; saw; sin/
  v. makita; nakita; nakita
see off /si AWF/ v. ihatid,
  despedidahin
seed /sid/ n. buto, binhi;
  v. binhian
seem /sim/ v. mukha
seize /siz/ v. dakmain
seldom /SEL-dam/ adv. bihira
self /saelf/ n. sarili
selfish /SEL-fish/ adj. maramot, makasarili

sell; sold; sold /sael; sold;
 sold/ v. ipagbili; ipinag-
 bili; nabili na
sell out /sael AWT/ v. nabili lahat
seller /SAEL-ar/ n. taga-
 pagtinda
send; sent; sent /saend;
 saent; saent/ v. ipadala;
 naipadala; naipadala
sense /saens/ n. isipan, u-
 lirat, dilidili; v. dili-
 diliin
sensible /SAENS-a-bol/ adj.
 matinis, matino
sentence /SAEN-tans/ n. talata; v. maghatol
separate /SAE-pa-ret/ v. hiwalayan; adj. bukod
separation /sae-pa-RE-syan/
 n. paghiwalay
September /Saep-TEM-bor/ n.
 Setyembre
serious /SIR-i-as/ adj. masinsinan, malubha

seriously /SIR-i-as-li/
 adv. grabe
servant /SUR-vant/ n. alila,
 alipin
serve /serv/ v. maglingkod,
 ihain
service /SUR-ves/ n. lingkod
service-station /SUR-ves
 ste-syan/ n. himpilan
set; set; set /saet; saet;
 saet/ v. ilagay; nilagay;
 nilagay; n. tangkas
settle /SAE-tol/ v. tuosin
settlement /SAE-tol-mant/
 n. tuos
settler /SAET-lar/ n. bagu-
 han
seven /SAE-van/ num. pito
seventeen /sae-van-TIN/
 num. labimpito
seventy /SAE-van-ti/ num.
 pitumpu
several /SAEV-or-al/ adj.
 ilan
severe /sa-VIR/ adj. grabe

sew; sewed; sewn /so; sod;
 son/ v. tahiin; tinahi;
 tinahi
shade /shed/ n. lilim; v.
 liliman
shadow /SHAE-do/ n. anino,
 aninag; v. nubok, manman
shake; shook; shaken /shek;
 shuok; SHE-kan/ v. alugin;
 kinalog; kinalog; n. uga,
 yugyog
shall /shael/ v. ay gagawin
shallow /SHAE-lo/ adj. mababaw; n. babaw
shame /shem/ n. hiya; v. hiyain
shape /shep/ n. hugis, hubog; v. hugisan, hubugin
share /sher/ v. paghati-
 hatiin; n. bakas, bahagi
sharp /sharp/ adj. matalas,
 matalim
shave /shev/ v. ahitan; n.
 ahit
she /shi/ prn. siya

sheep /ship/ n. tupa
sheet /shit/ n. kumot
shelf /shelf/ n. istante
shell /shael/ n. kabibi
shelter /SHAEL-tar/ n. habong; v. kumanlong
shield /shild/ n. kalasag,
  dangga; v. kalasagin
shine; shone; shone /shayn;
  shon; shon/ v. pakislapin;
  napakislap; napakislap; n.
  kislap, ningning
ship /shayp/ n. barko, bapor; v. ipadala
shipment /SHIP-mant/ n. padala
shirt /shurt/ n. kamisadentro
shock /shak/ n. gitla; v. gu-
  mimbal, biglain, gitlain
shoe /shu/ n. sapatos
shoot; shot; shot /shut;
  shat; shat/ v. barilin;
  binaril; nabaril
shop /shap/ v. mamili; n.
  tindahan

shore /shor/ n. pampang
short /short/ adj. maikli
shorts /shorts/ n. salawal
shortly /SHORT-li/ adv. mamayang kaunti
should /shud/ v. dapat
shoulder /SHOL-dar/ n. balikat; v. balikatin
shout /shawt/ v. hiyawan, bulyawan; n. hiyaw
show /sho/ n. tanghal; v. tanghalin
shower /SHAW-ar/ n. dutsa, ligo, anggi; v. maligo
shut /shat/ v. sarahan; adj. nasara
shut down /shat DAWN/ v. isara, ipinid; n. welga
sick /sik/ adj. may sakit
side /sayd/ n. piling, tabi, panig; v. panigan
sight /sayt/ n. paningin, tanaw; v. tumingin, tanawin
sign /sayn/ v. pirmahan, lagdaan; n. hudyat, karatula

signal /SIG-nal/ n. palahudyatan; v. hudyatan

silence /SAY-lans/ n. katahimikan; v. pahintuin

silent /SAY-lant/ adj. walang kibo

silk /silk/ n. sutla; adj.
sutlain

silver /SIL-var/ n. pilak;
adj. mapilak

simple /SIM-pol/ adj. simple, payak

simplicity /sem-PLIS-a-ti/
n. kahinhinan

simply /SIM-pli/ adv. basta

since /sins/ adv. mula;
conj. buhat

sincere /saen-SIR/ adj. taimtim, mataos, wagas

sing; sang; sung /sing;
saeng; sang/ v. awitin;
umawit; inawitan

single /SIN-gol/ adj. solo

singly /SIN-gli/ adv. isa't-
isa

sink; sank; sunk /sink;
 saenk; sank/ v. ilubog;
 lumubog; naglubog; n. la-
 babo
sir /sur/ n. ho, po, ginoo
sit; sat; sat /sit; saet;
 saet/ v. maupo; umupo; na-
 upo
situation /si-chu-E-syan/
 n. kalagayan
six /six/ num. anim
sixteen /six-TIN/ num. labing-anim
sixty /SIX-ti/ num. animnapu
size /sayz/ n. laki; v. sukatan
skill /skil/ n. kakayahan
skillful /SKIL-fol/ adj.
 mahusay
skin /skin/ n. balat
skirt /skirt/ n. palda
sky /skay/ n. langit, himpapawid
slave /slev/ n. busabos, a-
 lipin; v. lamayin

slavery /SLEV-or-i/ n. pag-
busabos

sleep; slept; slept /slip;
slaept; slaept/ v. matulog;
natulog; natulog; n. tulog

slide; slid; slid /slayd;
slid; slid/ v. dausdos; dumausdos; dumausdos; n. pag-
dausdos

slight /slayt/ adj. kapiranting; v. alipustain

slightly /SLAYT-li/ adv. bahagya

slip /slip/ n. tilas, dulas;
v. nadulas, lusutan

slope /slop/ n. libis, gulod;
v. libisan

slow /slo/ adj. mabagal, banayad; v. inot-inutan

slowly /SLO-li/ adv. dahan-
dahan

small /smal/ adj. maliit

smell; smelled; smelled
/smel; smeld; smeld/ v. a-
muyin; naamoy; naamoy; n.
amoy, anghit

smile /smayl/ v. ngitian;
n. ngiti
smoke /smok/ n. aso, usok;
v. sigaan, hithitin, umusok
smoker /SMO-kar/ n. manghi-
hitit
smooth /smuth/ adj. patag,
makinis; v. kayasin, buli
snake /snek/ n. ahas
sneeze /sniz/ v. bumahin;
n. bahin
snooze /snuz/ v. umidlip;
n. idlip
snore /snor/ v. hilik
snow /sno/ n. busilak; v.
magyelo
snowy /SNO-wi/ adj. mayelo
so /so/ adv. tapos; ex. pala
so-called /SO-kald/ adj. i-
yon ang tawag, ang tawag
doon
soap /sop/ n. sabon; v. sabunin
social /SO-syal/ adj. panli-
punan; n. pakikipagkapwa

society /so-SAY-a-ti/ n. lipunan, samahan, kapisanan
soft /sawft/ adj. malambot,
malambing
soften /SAW-fan/ v. palambutin
soil /soyl/ n. dalatan, lupa; v. dumihan
soldier /SOL-jar/ n. kawal,
sundalo
solemn /SA-lom/ adj. matindi
solid /SA-lid/ adj. matigas;
n. sikiin
solidarity /sal-i-DER-a-ti/
n. samahan
solution /so-LU-syan/ n.
kalutasan
solve /salv/ v. lutasin
some /som/ adj., adv. ilan
somebody /SAM-ba-di/ prn.
sinuman
somehow /SOM-haw/ adv. kahit
papaano
something /SOM-theng/ n. kuwan

sometimes /SOM-tayms/ adv.
 kung minsan
somewhat /SOM-hwat/ adv.
 mga, kaunting
son /san/ n. anak na lalaki
song /sawng/ n. awit, kanta
son-in-law /SAN in law/ n.
 manugang
soon /sun/ adv. malapit na
sore /sor/ adj. makirot;
 n. sugat
sorrow /SA-ro/ n. dalamhati,
 pighati, lumbay
sort /sort/ n. uri; v. pag-
 hiwa-hiwalay
soul /sol/ n. kaluluwa, diwa
sound /sawnd/ n. tunog, ingay; v. ingayan; adj. matatag
soup /sup/ n. sabaw
sour /sawr/ adj. maasim;
 v. nangasim
south /sawth/ n. timog;
 adv. sa timog
southern /SA-thern/ adj. ti-
 mugang

sow; sowed; sown /so; sod;
 son/ v. binhian; bininhi;
 bininhi
space /spes/ n. puwang;
 v. laktawan
spade /sped/ n. pala
spare /sper/ n. kapalit;
 adj. pampalit
speak; spoke; spoken /spik;
 spok; SPO-kan/ v. salitain;
 nagsalita; nagsalita
speaker /SPI-kar/ n. mana-
 nalumpati
special /SPE-syal/ adj. tangi, espesyal
specially /SPE-sya-li/ adv.
 na espesyal, na bago
speech /spich/ n. talumpati
speed; sped; sped /spid;
 spaed; spaed/ v. bilisan;
 bumilis; bumilis; n. bilis
spell; spelled; spelled
 /spael; spaeld; spaeld/ v.
 baybayin; binaybay; binaybay

spelling /SPAEL-eng/ n. bay-
 bay
spend; spent; spent /spaend;
 spaent; spaent/ v. gastus-
 in; gumasta; gumasta
spill; spilled; spilled
 /spil; spild; spild/ v. na-
 tapon; naitapon; naitapon;
 n. taob
spin; spun; spun /spin; span;
 span/ v. ikutin; naiikot;
 naiikot; n. ikot
spirit /SPIR-at/ n. diwa
spit; spat; spat /spit;
 spaet; spaet/ v. luraan;
 nilura; nilura; n. lura
spite /spayt/ n. buwisit;
 v. buwisitin
splendid /SPLEN-did/ adj.
 magaling
split; split; split /split;
 split; split/ v. biyakin;
 biniyak; biniyak; n. biyak
spoil; spoiled; spoiled
 /spoyl; spoyld; spoyld/ v.
 bulukin; nabulok; nabulok

spoon /spun/ n. kutsara
sport /sport/ n. palakasan
spot /spat/ n. batik; v. ba-
tikan
spread; spread; spread
/spraed; spraed; spraed/
v. ikadkad; kinadkad; nai-
kadkad; n. latag
spring; sprang; sprung
/spring; spraeng; sprang/
v. igkas; umigkas; umigkas;
n. batis, paigkas, balintang
square /skwer/ n. parisukat;
adj. kwadrado
staff /staef/ n. tungkod,
mga kagawad; v. maglagay ng
mga kawani
stage /stej/ n. entablado;
v. ipalabas
stain /sten/ n. mantsa, bahid; v. pulaan
stair /ster/ n. hagdan
staircase /STER-kes/ n. hagdanan
stamp /staemp/ n. selyo, ta-
tak; v. tatakan

stand; stood; stood /staend;
 stud; stud/ v. tayo; tumayo; tumayo; n. tindig, tayuan
standard /STAEN-dard/ adj.
 wasto; n. pamantayan
star /star/ n. bituin, artista; v. magartista; adj.
 pambato
start /start/ v. umpisahan;
 n. umpisa
state /stet/ n. bayan; adj.
 pangbansa; v. sabihin
statement /STET-mant/ n. lahad, hanay-ulat
statesman /STETS-man/ n.
 palabanwa
station /STE-syan/ n. himpilan, hintayan; v. humimpil
stay /ste/ v. manatili; n.
 pagtira
steadily /STAED-a-li/ adv.
 panay, unti-unti
steady /STAE-di/ adj. matatag

steal; stole; stolen /stil;
 stol; STO-lan/ v. nakawin;
 ninakaw; ninakaw
steam /stim/ n. singaw; v.
 sumingaw
steamer /STI-mar/ n. barko
steel /stil/ n. bakal
steep /stip/ adj. tarik; v.
 ibabad, inin
steer /stir/ v. rendahin
stem /staem/ n. tangkay;
 v. sangahin
step /staep/ n. hakbang, bay-
 tang; v. humakbang
stick; stuck; stuck /stik;
 stak; stak/ v. bumara; nagbara; nagbara; n. sanga
stiff /stif/ adj. matigas
still /stil/ adv. pa; adj.
 tahimik; v. patigilin
sting; stung; stung /sting;
 stang; stang/ v. sundot;
 nasundot; nasundot; n. hilam, kagat
stir /stur/ v. haluin; n.
 halo

stock /stak/ n. imbak; v.
 imbakin
stocky /STAK-i/ adj. mataba
stomach /STO-mek/ n. tiyan;
 v. nakakatiis
stone /ston/ n. bato; adj.
 gawang bato; v. pinukol
stony /STON-i/ adj. mabato
stop /stap/ v. pigilin; n.
 hinto, himpil
store /stor/ n. tindahan,
 tipon; v. tipunin
storm /storm/ n. bagyo; v.
 bumagyo
stormy /STOR-mi/ adj. mabag-
 yo
story /STOR-i/ n. kuwento,
 hikayat, palapag
stove /stov/ n. kalan, lutuan
straight /stret/ adj. matwid, ladlad
strange /strenj/ adj. kakaiba
stranger /STREN-jar/ n. dayuhan

strap /straep/ n. sakbit
straw /stra/ n. dayami
stream /strim/ n. saluysoy;
 v. umagos
street /strit/ n. daan
strength /strength/ n. lakas
stretch /straetch/ v. magi-
 nat; n. inat
strict /strikt/ adj. mahigpit
strictly /STRIKT-li/ adv.
 mahigpit na
strike; struck; stricken
 /strayk; strak; STRI-kan/
 v. hampasin; hinampas; hinampas; n. welga, aklasan
string /string/ n. pisi, tali; v. talian
strip /strip/ n. himulmol;
 v. hubaran
stripes /strayps/ n. pl.
 guhit-guhit
stroke /strok/ v. paluin;
 n. palo
strong /strang/ adj. malakas

struggle /STRA-gol/ v. lumaban; n. pakikibaka, piglas
study /STA-di/ v. magaral;
n. pinagaralan
stuff /stof/ n. bagay-bagay;
v. isaksak
stupid /STU-ped/ adj. tanga;
n. bobo
subject /SAB-jekt/ n. paksa;
v. mahirapan
substance /SAB-stans/ n.
sangkap
subway /SAB-we/ n. tren pang-
ilalim
succeed /sok-SID/ v. magwagi
success /sok-SES/ n. tagumpay, kasikatan
successful /sok-SES-fal/
adj. mapagtagumpay
successfully /sok-SES-fa-li/
adv. naipagtagumpay
such /sach/ prn., adj. ganyan, ganoon
suddenly /SA-dan-li/ adv.
biglaan

suffer /SA-for/ v. tiisin
sugar /SHU-gor/ n. asukal;
 v. tamisan
suggest /sag-JEST/ v. payuhan
suggestion /sag-JES-tyan/
 n. mungkahi
suit /sut/ n. bihis; v. bi-
nagayan
Summer /SA-mor/ n. taginit
sun /san/ n. araw; v. mag-
papaaraw
Sunday /SAN-de/ n. Linggo
sunshine /SAN-shayn/ n.
 sinag-araw
supper /SA-por/ n. hapunan
supply /sa-PLAY/ v. tustusan; n. sangkapin, gamitin
support /sa-PORT/ v. suhayan,
gabayan, tangkilikin, halig-
ihan; n. suhay, tangkilik,
tukod
suppose /sa-POZ/ v. sapan-
tahahin
sure /syur/ adj. tiyak, sigurado, nakasisiguro

surely /SYUR-li/ adv. pani-
guro
surface /SUR-fas/ n. dayad,
kalatagan; v. lumutang
surprise /sur-PRAYZ/ n. pag-
tataka, gulat, mangha; v.
mabigla, gulatin
surrender /so-RAEN-dar/ v.
sumuko; n. pagsuko
surround /su-RAWND/ v. ligiran, kulungin
suspect /sas-PEKT/ v. hinalain, kutuban; adj. mahinala
suspicion /sas-PI-syan/ n.
hinala
swallow /SWA-lo/ v. lulunin;
n. paglunok
swear; swore; sworn /swer;
swor; sworn/ v. sumpa; sumumpa; sumumpa
sweat /swaet/ v. pawisan;
n. pawis
sweep; swept; swept /swip;
swaept; swaept/ v. walisin;
winalis; nagwalis; n. walis

sweet /swit/ adj. matamis,
 matimyas
sweetly /SWIT-li/ adv. malambing
swell; swelled; swollen
 /swel; sweld; SWO-lan/ v.
 bukulan; bumukol; nakabukol
swelling /SWEL-eng/ n. maga,
 bukol, pantal
swim; swam; swum /swim;
 swaem; swam/ v. langoy; lumangoy; lumangoy; n. languyan
swindle /SWIN-dol/ v. dayain; n. pagdaya
swing; swang; swung /swing;
 swaeng; swang/ v. uguyin;
 inugoy; inugoy; n. duyan
sword /sord/ n. kampilan,
 kalis, itak
sympathetic /sim-pa-THAE-
 tik/ adj. nakikiramay
sympathy /SIM-pa-thi/ n.
 pakikiramay
system /SIS-tam/ n. kaayusan, pamamaraan

table   357   teach

table /TE-bol/ n. mesa, dulang; adj. pangmesa
tail /tel/ n. buntot; v.
sundan
tailor /TE-lor/ n. sastre;
v. sastrihan
take; took; taken /tek; tuk;
TE-kan/ v. kuhanin; kinu-
ha; kinuha
talk /tawk/ v. magusap; n.
salitaan, imik, daldal
tall /tawl/ adj. matangkad
tame /tem/ adj. maamo; v.
amuin
tap /taep/ v. katukin; n.
katok
taste /test/ v. tikman; n.
tikim, lasa, lasap
tax /taeks/ n. buwis; v. buwisan
taxi /TAEK-si/ n. taksi
tea /ti/ n. tsaa
teach; taught; taught /tich;
tawt; tawt/ v. turuan; tinuruan; tinuruan

teacher /TI-char/ n. guro
team /tim/ n. kuponan; v.
  itambal
tear; tore; torn /ter; tor;
  torn/ v. punitin; pinunit;
  pinunit; n. punit, sira
tease /tiz/ v. tuksuhin, bi-
  ruin; n. tukso
tedious /TID-i-as/ adj. matagal, mayamot
telegraph /TEL-a-graef/ n.
  pahatidkawad
telephone /TEL-a-fon/ n. te-
  lepono; v. tawagan
television /TEL-a-vis-yan/
  n. tanlap
tell; told; told /tael; told;
  told/ v. sabihin; sinabi;
  nagsabi
temper /TEM-por/ n. mainit
  ang ulo
temperature /TEM-pra-chur/
  temperatura
temple /TEM-pol/ n. templo,
  sintido

tempt /tempt/ v. tuksuhin
ten /taen/ num. sampu
tend /taend/ v. daluhan
tendency /TAEN-dan-si/ n.
 hilig
tender /TAEN-dor/ adj. malambing; v. binayaran
tent /taent/ n. kubol
term /tirm/ n. takda, kasali-
 taan, takay; v. itawag
terrible /TER-a-bol/ adj.
 kakila-kilabot
terribly /TER-a-bli/ adv.
 katakot-takot
test /taest/ n. subok; v.
 subukan, katiin
than /thaen/ conj. kaysa sa
thank /thaenk/ v. pasalamatin
thanks /thaenks/ n. salamat
thank you /THAENK yu/ ex.
 salamat
that /thaet/ prn., adj. iyan;
 conj. na
the /thi/ art. ang
theater /THI-a-tor/ n. dulaan

theirs /thers/ prn. kanilang
them /them/ prn. kanila
then /then/ adv. pagkatapos;
 conj. saka
there /ther/ adv. doon, diyan, hayan
therefore /THER-for/ adv.
 samakatuwid
these /thiz/ prn. pl. itong
 mga
thick /thik/ adj. makapal,
 malapot
thickness /THIK-nas/ n. kapal
thief /thif/ n. magnanakaw
thin /thin/ adj. payat; v.
 payatin, labnawin
thing /theng/ n. bagay, abubot
think; thought; thought
 /think; thawt; thawt/ v. i-
sipin; naisip; naisip
thirst /thurst/ n. uhaw; v.
 uhawin
thirsty /THURS-ti/ adj. nauhaw

thirteen /ther-TIN/ num.
 labintatlo
thirty /THER-ti/ num. tatlumpu
this /thaes/ prn., adj. ito
thorn /thorn/ n. tinik
thorough /THOR-o/ adj. ma-
 sinsin, lahatan
thoroughly /THOR-o-li/ adv.
 buong-buo
those /thoz/ prn. pl. iyong
 mga
though /tho/ conj. bagaman;
 adv. man
thought /thawt/ n. isip
thoughtful /THAWT-fol/ adj.
 maisip, mapagalala
thousand /THAW-zand/ num.
 libo
thread /thred/ n. sinulid,
 hibla; v. isinulot sa karayom
threaten /THRE-tan/ v. balaan
three /thri/ num. tatlo

throat /throt/ n. lalamunan
through /thru/ prep. labasan;
 adv. tapos
throw; threw; thrown /thro;
 thru; thron/ v. ihagis; i-
 nihagis; naihagis; n. hagis
thumb /thamb/ n. hinlalaki
thunder /THON-dar/ n. kulog;
 v. kumulog
Thursday /THARS-de/ n. Huwebes
thus /thas/ adv. ganito
ticket /TIK-et/ n. tiket
tide /tayd/ n. kati
tie /tay/ n. kurbata, gapos,
 buklod; v. gapusin, talian
tiger /TAY-gor/ n. tigre
tight /tayt/ adj. mahigpit,
 pitis
tighten /TAY-ton/ v. hig-
 pitan
till /til/ prep. hanggang;
 v. araruhin, asarolin,
 bungkalin
tilt /tilt/ n. tabingi

time /taym/ n. panahon, o-
ras; v. orasan
tin /tin/ n. tinggaputi, lata; adj. di lata
tip /tip/ n. pinakapuno, pabuya; v. magpabuya
tire /tayr/ n. gulong; v.
pagurin, pagalin
tired /TAY-ard/ adj. pagod,
pagal, handusay
title /TAY-tol/ n. pamagat
to /tu/ prep. sa
tobacco /tu-BAE-ko/ n. tabako
today /tu-DE/ adv., n. ngayong araw
toe /to/ n. daliri ng paa
together /tu-GAE-thar/ adv.
magkasabay
tomorrow /tu-MA-ro/ adv., n.
bukas
ton /tan/ n. tonelada
tongue /tang/ n. dila
tonight /tu-NAYT/ adv., n.
mamayang gabi
too /tu/ adv. rin, din, pati

tool /tul/ n. kasangkapan
tooth /tuth/ n. ngipin
top /tap/ n. ibabaw, taluktok; adj. pangibabaw
torture /TOR-chur/ n. pagpa-
pahirap; v. pinahirapan
total /TO-tal/ n. kabuuan,
katuusan; adj. buong, su-
mang; v. sumahan
touch /tach/ v. hipuin; n.
hipo
tough /taf/ adj. makunat,
magayot
tour /tur/ v. maglibot; n.
libot
tourist /TUR-est/ n. turista
towards /tords/ prep. sa
bandang
towel /TA-wol/ n. tuwalya
tower /TAW-ar/ n. tore, moog;
v. torehan
town /tawn/ n. pablasyon,
kabayanan
toy /toy/ n. laruan; v. laruin

track /traek/ n. bakas, riles, daambakal; v. matunton
trade /tred/ v. baliwasin;
n. baliwasan
trader /TRE-dar/ n. mangangalakal
traffic /TRAE-fik/ n. traf-
iko
trail /trel/ n. landas; v.
landasin
train /tren/ n. tren; v. sanayin
traitor /TRE-tor/ n. kuhila
translate /TRANS-let/ v. halawin, salin
translation /trans-LE-syan/
n. halaw
trap /traep/ n. patibong,
bitag; v. bitagin
travel /TRAE-vol/ v. lakbayin; n. paglalakbay
tray /tre/ n. bandeha, wataw
treasure /TRAES-yur/ n. yaman
treasurer /TRAES-yur-or/ n.
ingat-yaman

treat /trit/ v. tratuhin,
  gamutin, "magblo-out"
treatment /TRIT-mant/ n. pag-
  trato, gamutan
tree /tri/ n. puno
tremble /TREM-bol/ v. nginig, kilabutan, ngaligkig
trend /traend/ n. pagsulong
trial /TRAY-ol/ n. paglilitis; adj. pansubok
tribe /trayb/ n. kampon
trick /trik/ n. salamangka,
  lansihan; v. lansihin
trip /trip/ n. pasyal; v.
  patirin
trouble /TRA-bol/ n. ligalig; v. ligaligin
trousers /TRAW-sars/ n. pl.
  mga salawal
truce /trus/ n. pagkakasun-
  duan
truck /trok/ n. trak
true /tru/ adj. totoo
truly /TRU-li/ adv. nga
trunk /trank/ n. baol

trust /trast/ n. tiwala;
 v. maniwala
truth /truth/ n. katotohanan
truthful /TRUTH-fol/ adj.
 matapat
try /tray/ v. subukin; n.
 subok
tub /tab/ n. batya
tube /tub/ n. tubo
Tuesday /TUS-de/ n. Martes
tuition /tu-IS-yan/ n. ma-
 trikula
tune /tun/ n. himig; v. i-
 tono
tune in /tun IN/ v. buksan
 ang
tune up /tun AP/ v. ikun-
 disyon
turkey /TUR-ki/ n. pabo
turn /turn/ v. pihitin; n.
 pihit, liko
turn back /turn BAEK/ v.
 bumalik
turn off /turn AWF/ v. patayin

turn on /turn AN/ v. buksan

twelve /twelv/ num. labindalawa

twenty /TWEN-ti/ num. dalawampu

twice /tways/ adv. makalawa

twin /twin/ n. kambal

twist /twist/ v. pilipitin;
n. pilipit

two /tu/ num. dalawa

type /tayp/ n. uri; v. makin-
ilyahin

typical /TIP-a-kol/ adj. karaniwan

ugly /AG-li/ adj. pangit

ultimate /AL-ti-mat/ adj.
ang pinaka

umbrella /am-BRE-la/ n. payong

unable /an-E-bol/ adj. di-
kaya

unacceptable /an-aek-SEP-ta-
bol/ adj. hindi-matatanggap

unarmed /on-ARMD/ adj. na
walang armas

unbutton /an-BAT-on/ v. tanggalin ang butones
uncle /AN-kol/ n. tiyo, a-
  main
unconscious /on-KAN-syas/
  adj. bulagta, walang malay
unconsciousness /on-KAN-
  syas-nas/ n. pagkabulagta
under /ON-dar/ prep. ilalim;
  adv. sa ilalim
underneath /on-der-NITH/
  adv. sa ilalim
understand; understood; understood /on-der-STAEND; on-
  der-STUD; on-der-STUD/ v.
  unawain; naunawaan; naunawaan
understandable /on-der-STAEN-
  da-bol/ adj. maunawain
unemployment /on-em-PLOY-
  mant/ n. walang hanapbuhay
unfasten /an-FAES-an/ v. ka-
  lagin
unfold /an-FOLD/ v. iladlad
uniform /YU-na-form/ n. uni-
  porme

union /YUN-yan/ n. samahan
unique /yu-NIK/ adj. ka-
  tangi-tangi
unit /YUN-it/ n. isahan
unite /yu-NAYT/ v. umanib,
  buklurin
unity /YUN-a-ti/ n. kaisahan
universal /yun-a-VAER-sol/
  adj. sansinukbin
universe /YUN-a-vaers/ n.
  sansinukob
university /yun-i-VAERS-a-
  ti/ n. pamantasan
unjust /on-JAST/ adj. di-
  husto
unless /on-LAES/ conj. kundi
unlikely /on-LAYK-li/ adj.
  hindi naman siguro
unpack /on-PAEK/ v. kalagan
unpaid /on-PED/ adj. di-
  sinuswelduhan
unpleasant /on-PLE-sant/
  adj. masaklap
unreliable /on-ri-LAY-a-bol/
  adj. di-maasahan

unrest /on-REST/ n. gulo
unsatisfactory /on-sae-tis-
  FAEK-tor-i/ adj. di kasiya-
  siya
untidy /on-TAY-di/ adj. busalsal
until /an-TIL/ prep., conj.
  hanggang
unwilling /on-WIL-eng/ adj.
  ayaw
up /ap/ adv. sa ibabaw
up to /ap TU/ prep. hanggang
upon /a-PAN/ prep. sa ibabaw ng
upper /AP-or/ adj. pangitaas
upright /AP-rayt/ adj. ka-
  tayo; adv. nakatayo
uprising /OP-ray-seng/ n.
  himagsikan
upset /op-SAET/ adj. nainis;
  v. inisin
upside-down /op-sayd DAWN/
  adv. patiwarik
upstairs /ap-STERS/ adv. i-
  taas

up-to-date /ap-tu-DET/ adj.
 makabago
upwards /AP-words/ adv. salunga
urge /erj/ v. sulsulan, udyukan; n. sulsol, udyok
urgent /UR-jant/ adj. nagmamadali
urine /YU-rin/ n. ihi
use /yuz/ v. gamitin; n.
 gamit
used /yuzd/ adj. galgal
useful /YUS-fol/ adj. mapakinabang
useless /YUS-las/ adj. laos
usher /ASH-ur/ n. tagahatid
usual /YUZ-u-al/ adj. karaniwan
usually /YUZ-ya-li/ adv. ka-
 raniwang pangyayari
vacant /VE-kant/ adj. walang
 nakatira, walang tao
vacation /ve-KES-yan/ n.
 bakasyon
vaccinate /VAEKS-o-net/ v.
 magkulantro

vaccination /vaeks-in-E-syan/
n. kulantro
vague /veg/ adj. malabo
vain /ven/ adj. banidoso
valid /VAE-lid/ adj. di-
huwad
valley /VAEL-li/ n. libis
valuable /VAEL-ya-bol/ adj.
mahalaga
value /VAEL-yu/ n. halaga;
v. kahalagahan
vanish /VAEN-esh/ v. mawala,
mapawi
vanity /VAEN-a-ti/ n. kalokohan
variety /va-RAY-a-ti/ n.
sari-sari
various /VER-i-as/ adj.
iba't-ibang
vault /valt/ v. luksuhin;
n. lukso, kahadiyero
vegetable /VAEJ-ta-bol/
n. gulay
vehicle /VI-hay-kol/ n.
sasakyan

veil /vel/ n. kulubong, ku-
  bong; v. nagkulubong
verb /vurb/ n. pandiwa
vernacular /vur-NAEK-yu-lar/
  n., adj. salitang kalye
verse /vurs/ n. tugma, taludtod
vertical /VUR-ti-kal/ adj.
  paakyat
very /VE-ri/ adv. napaka
vessel /VAES-al/ n. lalagyan, lagyanan
vicinity /vi-SAEN-a-ti/ n.
  pook
vicious /VIS-yas/ adj. asal-
  hayop
victim /VIK-tom/ n. biktima
victor /VIK-tor/ n. siyang
  nanalo
victorious /vik-TOR-i-as/
  pananagumpay
victory /VIK-to-ri/ n. tagumpay
view /viw/ n. tanawin; v.
  manood

village /VIL-aj/ n. baryo
violence /VAY-o-lens/ n.
 basag-ulo, dahas
violent /VAY-o-lant/ adj.
 mabagsik
viper /VAY-par/ n. ahas
virtue /VER-chu/ n. bait
virus /VAY-ras/ n. haykap,
 mikrobyo
visibility /vis-a-BIL-a-ti/
 n. pagkahalata
visit /VIS-at/ v. dalawin;
 n. dalaw
visitor /VIS-i-tar/ n. panauhin
vitamin /VAY-ta-min/ n.
 bitamina
vogue /vog/ n. moda
voice /voys/ n. tinig; v.
 magsabi
void /voyd/ n. kawalan; v.
 kalasin; adj. kalas
volume /VAL-yum/ n. buok
vomit /VA-mit/ v. duwal;
 n. suka

vote /vot/ v. iboto; n. boto, halal
voucher /VAW-chur/ n. kapatunayan
voyage /VOY-aj/ n. paglalakbay
vulgar /VAL-gor/ adj. magaslaw, bulastog, haliparot
vulnerable /VOL-ner-a-bol/
adj. nakatunganga
wage /wej/ n. sahod, upahan
waist /west/ n. baywang
wait /wet/ v. maghintay;
n. hintay
waiting room /WET-eng rum/
n. hintayan
waitress /WET-ras/ n. tagapagsilbi
wake; woke; woken /wek; wok;
WO-kan/ v. gisingin; nagising; nagising
wake up /wek AP/ v. gisingin, pukawin
walk /wawk/ v. lakarin;
n. lakad

walk out /wawk AWT/ v. tinalikuran

walk over /wawk O-var/ v. pumarini

walker /WAK-or/ n. tungkod

wall /wal/ n. dingding

wander /WAN-dor/ v. layas

want /want/ v. gusto, ibigin; n. nais

war /wor/ n. digma; v. digmain

ward /word/ n. ampon, alaga; v. itaboy

wardrobe /WORD-rob/ n. aparador

warehouse /WER-haws/ n. bodega

warm /worm/ adj. mainit; v. initin

warmth /wormth/ n. init

warn /worn/ v. balaan, babalaan

warning /WORN-eng/ n. pauna, babala

wary /WER-i/ adj. nagaalaala

wash /wash/ v. labhan; n.
  nilalabahan
wash and wear /wash aynd
  WER/ n. labhan at isuot
washing machine /WASH-eng
  ma-shin/ n. labahan
waste /west/ n. sayang; v.
  aksaya
watch /watch/ n. rilos, bantay; v. bantayan
watchmaker /WATCH-me-kor/
  n. relohero
water /WA-tor/ n. tubig;
  v. diligin
watermelon /WA-tor-me-lan/
  n. pakuwan
waterproof /WA-tor-pruf/
  adj. di-tinatalaban ng
  tubig
wave /wev/ v. kaway, kulutin;
  n. alon, kulot
wavy /WEV-i/ adj. makulot
wax /waeks/ n. pagkit;
  adj. lagkit
way /we/ n. paraan

we /wi/ prn. tayo, kami
weak /wik/ adj. mahina, lam-
pa, marupok
weaken /WI-kan/ v. lampahin
weakness /WIK-nas/ n. hina
wealth /welth/ n. kayamanan
wealthy /WEL-thi/ adj. mayaman
weapon /WAE-pan/ n. armas
wear; wore; worn /wer; wor;
worn/ v. isuot; sinuot;
nagsuot; n. suot, gasgas
wear off /wer AUF/ v. na-
bakbak
weary /WIR-i/ adj. lugmok,
hapo, handusay
weather /WE-thar/ n. panahon
weave /wiv/ v. habiin
wedding /WED-eng/ n. kasal;
adj. pangkasal
Wednesday /WENS-de/ n. Miyerkoles
weed /wid/ n. damu-damo;
v. tinutungkab
week /wik/ n. linggo

weekly /WIK-li/ adj. lingguhan; adv. linggu-linggo
weep; wept; wept /wip;
  waept; waept/ v. iyak; u-
  miyak; umiyak; n. hagulgol,
  panaghoy
weigh /we/ v. timbangin
weight /wet/ n. timbang,
  bigat, pataw
weird /wird/ adj. pambihira
welcome /WEL-kam/ n. bati;
  v. batiin; ex. pasok kayo
well /wel/ n. balon; adj.
  mabuti
well-being /wel-BI-eng/ n.
  kabutihan
west /west/ n. kanluran;
  adv. sa kanluran
western /WES-tarn/ adj. kan-
  lurang
wet /waet/ adj. basa; v. basain, lawain
what /hwat/ int. ano
whatever /hwat-E-var/ adj.
  kahit ano, anuman

wheat /hwit/ n. trigo
wheel /hwil/ n. gulong;
 v. pagulungin
when /hwaen/ adv., int. kailan; conj. nang
whenever /hwaen-E-var/ adv.
 kailan man
where /hwer/ adv., int. saan;
 conj. nasaan
wherever /hwer-AE-var/ adv.
 kahit saan, saan man
whether /HWAE-thar/ conj.
 kung
which /hwich/ adv., int. a-
 lin; conj. na, na siya
while /hwayl/ conj. habang,
 samantalang; n. muna, sandali
whip /hwip/ n. latiko; v.
 latikuhin
whipped cream /hwipt KRIM/
 n. sinabol na krema
whisper /HWIS-por/ v. bu-
 lungin; n. bulong
whistle /HWIS-al/ v. sutsutan; n. sutsot, pasiyok

white /hwayt/ adj. maputi;
n. puti
who /hu/ prn., int. sino
whoever /hu-E-var/ prn. kahit sino, sino man
whole /hol/ adj. buo; n. kabuuan
wholesale /HOL-sel/ adj. ma-
ramihan; n. pakyaw; v. pakyawin
whom /hum/ prn. kanino
whose /huz/ prn., int. kanino
why /hway/ adv., int. bakit,
ba't
wicked /WIK-ed/ adj. salbahe
wide /wayd/ adj. malapad,
malawak
widely /WAYD-li/ adv. nakakalat
widow /WI-do/ n. biyuda
width /width/ n. lapad
wife /wayf/ n. asawang babae
wig /wig/ n. piluka
wild /wayld/ adj. mabangis

will /wil/ n. habilin; v.
  magbilin
willing /WIL-eng/ adj. mahilig
win; won; won /win; wan; wan/
  v. magwagi; nagwagi; nagwagi
wind /wind/ n. hangin; v.
  susian
winding /WAYND-eng/ adj.
  pulupot
window /WIN-do/ n. bintana,
  durungawan
windshield /WIND-shild/ n.
  bintanang kotse
wine /wayn/ n. alak
wing /wing/ n. pakpak, bag-
  wis
winner /WI-nar/ n. nanalo
winter /WIN-tor/ n. taglamig, tagulan
wipe /wayp/ v. punasan
wipe off /wayp AUF/ v. pagpagin, pahirin

wire /wayr/ n. kawad, alam-
  bre; v. ipahatid kawad
wisdom /WIS-dam/ n. karu-
  nungan
wise /wayz/ adj. matalino,
  maalam
wish /wish/ v. naisin; n.
  nais, lunggati
wit /wit/ n. uluhan
witch /witch/ n. asuwang
with /with/ prep. kalakip,
  at nang
within /with-IN/ prep. loob
  ng; adv. sa loob
without /with-AWT/ prep. na
  walang
witness /WIT-nas/ n. saksi;
  v. masaksihan
witty /WIT-i/ adj. komika
woe /wo/ n. hapis
wolf /wolf/ n. lobo
woman /WU-man/ n. babae
wonder /WON-dur/ n. pagtata-
  ka, gilalas; v. nagtataka
wood /wuod/ n. kahoy

wool /wul/ n. lana
woolen /WUL-an/ adj. lanilya
word /wurd/ n. salita
work; worked; worked /wurk;
 wurkd; wurkd/ v. magtrabaho;
 nagtrabaho; nagtrabaho; n.
 trabaho, pasok
worker /WURK-or/ n. mangga-
 gawa
world /wurld/ n. daigdig;
 adj. sandaigdigan, dutain
worm /wurm/ n. uod, bulati
worn-out /worn-AWT/ adj. gasgas na
worried /WOR-id/ adj. balisa
worry /WOR-i/ v. balisahin,
 magalala; n. pangamba, kaba,
 balino, balisa
worse /wurs/ adj. masahol;
 adv. masahol pa
worsen /WUR-san/ v. lumala
worship /WUR-ship/ v. sambahin, poonin; n. pagsamba
worst /wurst/ adj. pinakama-
 sahol

worth /wurth/ n. halaga, say-
  say; adj. may halaga
worthless /WURTH-las/ adj.
  walang kuwenta, bale wala
worthwhile /wurth-HWAYL/
  adj. marapatan, may kuwenta
would /wud/ v. ay gagawin
wound /wund/ n. sugat; v. sugatan
wrap /wraep/ v. balutin; n.
  balot, kulob, balabal
wreck /wrek/ v. gibain, wasakin; n. giba
wrench /wraench/ n. liyabe;
  v. liyabihin
wrestling /RAES-leng/ n. nag-
  bobono
wring; wrung; wrung /ring;
  rang; rang/ v. pilipitin;
  pinilipit; pinilipit
wrinkle /WRING-kol/ v. kulubutin; n. kulubot, kunot
wrist /wrist/ n. pulso
write; wrote; written /rayt;
  rot; WRIT-an/ v. sulatan;
  sumulat; nagsulat

write down /rayt DAWN/ v. i-
  tala
writer /WRAY-tor/ n. manunulat
wrong /wrong/ adj. mali, lis-
  ya; v. nalisya, apihin
wry /wray/ adj. mapang-uyam
yacht /yat/ n. yate
yard /yard/ n. yarda, ba-
  kuran
yawn /yawn/ v. humigab; n.
  higab
year /yir/ n. taon
yearly /YIR-li/ adj. taunan;
  adv. taon-taon
yell /yel/ v. hiyawan; n.
  hiyaw
yellow /YEL-o/ adj. dilaw;
  v. dilawin
yes /yes/ adv., ex. oo
yesterday /YES-tor-de/ n.,
  adv. kahapon
yet /yaet/ adv. pa; conj.
  subali't
yield /yild/ v. magtugot,
  sumuko; n. tugot, ani

yogurt /YO-gurt/ n. ginatan
you /yu/ prn. ikaw, ka; pl.
 kayo
young /yang/ adj. bata, musmos
your /yor/ adj. iyong, in-
 yong
yours /yors/ prn., adj. sa
 iyo, sa inyo
yourself /yor-SELF/ prn.
 sarili mo
yourselves /yor-SELVZ/ prn.
 sarili ninyo
youth /yuth/ n. kasibulan,
 kabataan
youths /yuths/ n. pl. mga
 kabataan
zero /ZI-ro/ n. sero
zipper /ZI-por/ n. siper
zone /zon/ n. pook, barangay
zoom /zum/ v. hagibis

ABBREVIATIONS - DAGLAT

adj. adjective - panguri
adv. adverb - pangabay
art. article - pantukoy
conj. conjunction - pangatnig
ex. exclamation or expression
            - pandamdam
int. interrogative -
            pangtanong
n. noun - pangngalan
num. numeral - bilang
part. particle - kataga
pl. plural - mga
prep. preposition - pangukol
prn. pronoun - panghalip
ref. term of address -
            pagalang
v. verb - pandiwa

Ilocano-English/English-Ilocano Dictionary and Phrasebook
by Carl R. Galvez Rubino, Ph.D.

The aim of this dictionary and phrasebook is to assist the student or traveler in expanding his or her knowledge of the language and culture of the Philippines.
- Introduction to basic grammar
- Pronunciation guide
- Ilocano-English/English-Ilocano dictionary
- Ilocano phrasebook

175 pages • 5 x 8 • 0-7818-0642-9 • W • $14.95pb • (718)

Tagalog-English/English-Tagalog (Pilipino) Standard Dictionary
by Carl R. Galvez Rubino, Ph.D.

This dictionary was written to serve two audiences: speakers of Tagalog who need access to a bilingual dictionary, and students of the Tagalog language. It is a comprehensive collection of over 20,000 words and includes idiomatic expressions, slang, loan words, and derivations. The English-Tagalog section includes a vocabulary appendix, a separate section discussing the affixes, and a grammatical overview explaining the intricacies of Tagalog.

300 pages • 6 x 9 • 20,600 entries • 0-7818-0657-7 • W • $14.95pb • (714)

Tagalog-English/English-Tagalog (Pilipino) Dictionary

With more than 10,000 entries, this dictionary is suitable for students and travelers alike.

500 pages • 5 x 8 • 10,000 entries • 0-7818-0683-6 • NA • $29.95hc • (745)

All prices subject to change. **To purchase Hippocrene Books** contact your local bookstore, call (718) 454-2366, or write to: HIPPOCRENE BOOKS, 171 Madison Avenue, New York, NY 10016. Please enclose check or money order, adding $5.00 shipping (UPS) for the first book and $.50 for each additional book.